Field Guide to
Seaweeds
of Alaska

Mandy R. Lindeberg
Sandra C. Lindstrom

Published by
Alaska Sea Grant College Program
University of Alaska Fairbanks

$30
SG-ED-69

Elmer E. Rasmuson Library Cataloging in Publication Data

Lindeberg, Mandy R.

Field guide to seaweeds of Alaska / Mandy R. Lindeberg ; Sandra C. Lindstrom. – Fairbanks, Alaska : Alaska Sea Grant College Program, University of Alaska Fairbanks, 2010.

p. : ill. ; cm. – (Alaska Sea Grant College Program, University of Alaska Fairbanks; SG-ED-69)

Includes bibliographical references and index.

1. Marine algae—Alaska—Guidebooks. 2. Green algae—Alaska—Guidebooks. 3. Brown algae—Alaska—Guidebooks. 4. Red algae—Alaska—Guidebooks. 5. Seagrasses—Alaska—Guidebooks. I. Title. II. Lindstrom, Sandra C. III. Series: Alaska Sea Grant College Program, University of Alaska Fairbanks; SG-ED-69.

QK571.5.A4 L56 2010   Second Printing 2015

ISBN 978-1-56612-156-9

http://doi.org/10.4027/fgsa.2010

Printed in China

Credits

This book is published by the Alaska Sea Grant College Program, supported by the U.S. Department of Commerce, NOAA National Sea Grant Office, grant NA10OAR4170097, project A/161-02; and by the University of Alaska Fairbanks with state funds. NOAA National Marine Fisheries Service, Alaska Fisheries Science Center, and the Cook Inlet Regional Citizens Advisory Council also provided support for publishing cost.

The University of Alaska is an affirmative action/equal opportunity employer and educational institution. For information on undergraduate and graduate opportunities in marine biology, fisheries, oceanography, and other marine-related fields at the University of Alaska Fairbanks School of Fisheries and Ocean Sciences, visit http://www.sfos.uaf.edu/.

Sea Grant is a unique partnership with public and private sectors combining research, education, and technology transfer for public service. This national network of universities meets changing environmental and economic needs of people in our coastal, ocean, and Great Lakes regions.

Book design, layout, and cover design by Jen Gunderson; project coordination by Kurt Byers; and project management and copyediting by Sue Keller, of Alaska Sea Grant. Cover photo shows golden V kelp (*Aureophycus aleuticus*), an endemic seaweed from the Aleutian Islands. Photo by Shawn Harper, University of Alaska Fairbanks Institute of Marine Science.

Alaska Sea Grant College Program
University of Alaska Fairbanks
P.O. Box 755040
Fairbanks, Alaska 99775-5040
Toll free (888) 789-0090
(907) 474-6707 • fax (907) 474-6285
www.alaskaseagrant.org

Table of Contents

About the authors

Mandy Lindeberg, a research biologist, has been conducting scientific research in Alaska since 1990. Her passion for seaweeds began while working for the University of Alaska Fairbanks and continues with NOAA Fisheries (National Oceanic and Atmospheric Administration) in Juneau, Alaska. Her research includes studies on intertidal invertebrates, seaweeds, bioavailability of contaminants in the nearshore, and coastal habitat mapping. These projects have taken her all over Alaska and enabled her to develop a diverse knowledge of Alaska seaweeds, including the discovery of a new kelp in the Aleutian Islands. Along the way she developed a joy for photography, resulting in the majority of photos found in this book.

Sandra Lindstrom, who was born and raised in Juneau, Alaska, has studied seaweeds in Alaska for over 35 years. She has an M.S. in marine biology and a Ph.D. in botany from the University of British Columbia. She has authored more than 60 scientific papers on seaweeds and is a coauthor of half a dozen books. She has taught courses in the biology of seaweeds in Alaska, British Columbia, and Washington state and is an active member of regional, national, and international phycological societies.

Acknowledgments

Support for this book was made possible by NOAA Fisheries, Auke Bay Laboratories, and the Alaska Sea Grant College Program. Also, the authors wish to thank those who reviewed this book: Dr. Michael Wynne, Dr. Paul Gabrielson, Marilyn Sigman, and Chiska Derr. Many of the species descriptions were aided by the book *North Pacific Seaweeds,* with permission from Rita O'Clair.

The photographic contributions to this book by the following people are gratefully appreciated: Reid Brewer, Heloise Chenelot, Roger Clark, Bill Driskell, Ken Dutton, Shawn Harper, Pat Harris, Stephen Jewett, Mary Morris, Fabio Rindi, Sue Saupe, and Johanna Vollenweider. Seaweeds can be challenging to photograph.

A special thanks goes to Susan Saupe with Cook Inlet Regional Citizens Advisory Council, who went beyond encouragement over many years to see this book published. She provided numerous opportunities and funding for the authors to explore remote coastlines of Alaska through her various projects.

Preface

Inspiration for this guide lies with the many people who visit Alaska's shoreline and their desire to learn more about seaweeds. It is designed so you do not have to be a seaweed expert and provides quick, accurate identifications in the field. We have selected over 100 species of seaweeds that occur in Alaska's coastal waters, some of which are unique to Alaska and are not found in other references. Short sections on seagrasses and marine lichens are also included. Many species in this book also commonly occur along the Pacific coast of North America, and you will find this guide useful throughout that area as well.

The seaweed species are organized into three taxonomic groups based on color (green, brown, and red) and then by their shape. To guide you through these classifications, quick keys (color and form) are provided, and the pages are color coded for fast navigation to a seaweed group. Each species has a complete yet brief description of taxonomy, distribution, appearance, habitat preferences, and similar taxa. This book is unique because it provides photographs of seaweeds in their natural habitat along with digitized scans of pressed herbarium specimens. The majority of photos and specimens in this book were collected by the authors throughout Alaska between 1990 and 2010.

We hope this book will help guide you into the wonderful world of seaweeds and foster an appreciation of them, as it has in the authors.

Using this guide

There are approximately 550 species of seaweeds known to occur in Alaska and, as we explore more of its remote coastline and discover previously unknown species, that number continues to grow. This book does not attempt to describe all of Alaska's seaweeds, but instead depicts over 100 common species, including a few that are endemic to Alaska. We have included a section at the end of each color group called occasional seaweeds, which briefly describes species that are not as common, only found in a specific area, or easily confused with other Alaska species. In addition, brief descriptions of Alaska seagrasses and marine lichens are near the end of the book.

The seaweeds are arranged in three color groups, and within these groups by their different forms. Pages are color coded, and quick pictorial keys are provided immediately before the Green Seaweeds section and at the beginning of each color section.

Follow these steps to identify a seaweed:

1. Go to the illustrations in a quick key to determine in which of the three main color groups it belongs:

   Green seaweeds (Chlorophyta), usually grass green or dark green.
   Brown seaweeds (Ochrophyta: Phaeophyceae), usually golden or chocolate brown.
   Red seaweeds (Rhodophyta), often pink, purple, red, or other colors.

2. Determine which common form your seaweed most resembles (crust, filament, blade, etc.) in that color group.

3. Turn to the page listed for that group and browse through the taxa to find the seaweed in question.

4. Cross reference your identification with similar to or occasional seaweeds that may be listed with the descriptions. Occasional seaweeds are located at the end of each color group.

5. Alternatively, if you know the color but are not sure what form it is or can't remember a species name, go directly to the beginning of the color group and use the quick key to find the species and page numbers to guide you to your seaweed.

For further information on seaweeds of Alaska visit www.seaweedsofalaska.com.

A word about color and form

Variability in color and form for a given species is a common problem in identifying seaweeds (Figure 1). One of the most frequent sources of error is selecting the proper color group. Factors such as freshwater, sunlight, nutrient deficiency, and reproductive activity can result in a seaweed losing pigment from its cells, which can dramatically alter its color. Red seaweeds are the most confusing. They commonly appear yellow, green, brown, or black instead of red. So, please keep an open mind when descriptions state coloration. The color near the base of the thallus is often the most consistent under changing conditions. In addition, different specimens of one species can vary in form due to environmental conditions. The common morphological groupings (by shape) listed in the quick keys are based on seaweeds having the same general shape or structural components. As with any system, there will be some specimens that do not fit, but these groupings generally work for the purposes of this guide.

Variable color and form

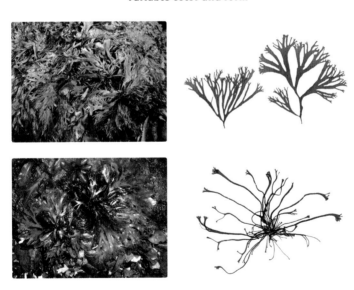

Figure 1. An example of the red alga *Palmaria callophylloides* with different coloration and form.

Using this guide

Nomenclature and taxonomy

For each species we provide a common name, scientific name, species authority, former scientific names, and taxonomic classification. A taxon (plural: taxa) is a unit in the classification of organisms, be it (in descending order of inclusiveness) phylum, class, order, family, genus, or species. Here is a quick lesson in botanical nomenclature:

- The three major groups of seaweeds are phyla (names ending in "-phyta").
- Each phylum is divided into classes (names ending in "-phyceae").
- Each class is divided into orders (ending in "-ales").
- Each order is divided into families (ending in "-aceae").
- Families are then divided into various genera and finally into species.

In addition, each scientific name is followed by the name of the author who first described the species (authority). If another scientist changed the original name, such as transferring the species to a different genus, the name of the author who first described the species is listed in parentheses, and the author of the currently accepted name follows. Nomenclature and taxonomy are by no means static, and as we learn more about seaweeds and their genetic makeup, scientific names change. This can be a source of frustration for all concerned, so we have listed synonyms or former names to ease the confusion. In some instances, an incorrect name was formerly used for a species. When this was the case, we list that name under "misidentified as."

Illustrations

Traditionally scientists preserve and archive seaweeds by drying them on paper, similar to flowering plants, for storage in a herbarium. Casual seaweed enthusiasts may not have access to a herbarium and may find it a struggle to identify a fresh specimen. This unique field guide presents digital scans of herbarium specimens and photos of the species in their natural habitat to further aid identification.

Distribution and descriptions

Although this is a field guide for Alaska, many species occur in adjacent regions. To keep it simple, we restrict distribution data to the North Pacific.

- **Distribution.** A map of Alaska with regional names is printed inside the back cover.

- **Description** narratives for each species touch on form, color, size, and unique structures as the species appear in Alaska waters (sizes may differ in other regions).

- A **glossary** of algal terms can be found near the end of the book.

- **Habitat** information includes preferred substrates, tidal zones, and exposure to wave energy. Almost all seaweeds are edible, some more palatable than others, and we do point out species that have commercial names.

- **Similar to** lists seaweeds that are easily confused with the species being described, and these should be checked before settling on an identification.

- An asterisk (*) indicates that a species can be found in the "occasional" species section.

- A cross (†) means that the species is not represented in this guide.

Know your way around the taxon page

Common name
Genus species (Original Authority) Authority

Former names *Genus species*

Class -phyceae

Order -ales

Family -aceae

North Pacific distribution Restricted to North Pacific but many species can be found beyond this distribution.

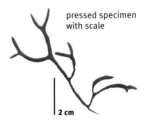

pressed specimen with scale

| 2 cm

Description Describes species appearance and if significant, reproductive strategy.

Habitat Describes general substrate, intertidal zone, and coastal exposure preference of this seaweed.

Similar to A list of other taxa that could be confused with this one.
* = species can be found in "occasional" species section. † = species is not represented in this guide.

What are seaweeds?

The phylogenetic tree in Figure 2 is a way of visualizing relationships among organisms based on evolutionary development. Algae are a heterogeneous group that includes diatoms and dinoflagellates as well as seaweeds. Seaweeds are divided into three main groups known as green (Chlorophyta), brown (class Phaeophyceae in phylum Ochrophyta), and red (Rhodophyta), the latter two groups containing pigments that mask the chlorophyll that all three groups possess as photosynthetic organisms. Detailed descriptions of these seaweed groups are presented at the beginning of each color section.

Important definitions: algae versus seaweeds

algae "al-jee" (plural); **alga** "al-guh" (singular): aquatic (freshwater and marine, rarely terrestrial) photosynthetic organisms ranging from unicellular to multicellular forms that generally lack the differentiated tissues found in most land plants.

microalgae: algae that are mostly unicellular and microscopic (such as dinoflagellates and diatoms).

macroalgae: macroscopic algae, known as **seaweeds** in the marine environment.

phycology: the study of algae. Derived from the Greek root phykos, which means seaweed.

Structure and function

Although seaweeds are photosynthesizers, they lack the anatomically complex roots, stems, branches, and leaves of most land plants. They do have analogous structures, which have similar functions. These seaweed structures often lack differentiated tissues and have their own terminology. An entire plant is called a **thallus**, a leaflike structure is a **blade**, a midvein is a **midrib**, a stem is a **stipe**, and a root-like structure that attaches the seaweed to the substrate is called a **holdfast**. Branching patterns are also an important component to seaweed identification (Figure 3). These basic structures have many variations among the seaweeds, resulting in a plethora of terminology describing seaweed shape, or morphology. We have tried to limit the use of these terms, but a glossary has also been provided in the book as an aid.

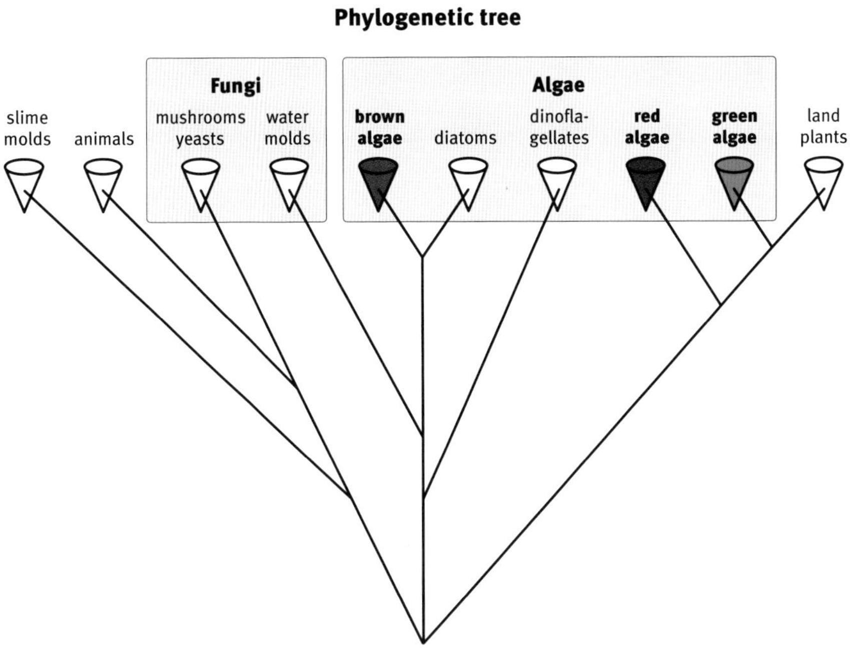

Phylogenetic tree

Figure 2. Phylogenetic tree from Keeling et al. 2005.

What are seaweeds?

Seaweeds have an amazing diversity of forms that serve various functions in the nearshore environment. A thallus can be a simple chain of single cells arranged in a linear **filament**, one or two layers of cells arranged in a sheetlike blade, or more complex forms of specialized cell layers such as an outer pigmented **cortex** and an inner colorless **medulla**. These forms, however, have some recurrent patterns that are a result of the challenging environment in which they have evolved. Thin blades acquire lots of energy from sunlight and grow very quickly. Thick blades, such as kelps, specialize in staying attached to substrates under enormous forces from waves but are slow growing. In general, as functional forms increase in complexity, their growth rates decline (Table 1).

Reproduction

Seaweeds are among the most complex and varied of groups regarding their life histories and reproductive strategies. Generally, seaweeds reproduce sexually when a fusion of gametes occurs, with meiosis (reduction division) usually following at a later time; hence there is an alternation of generations in their life cycle. The alternating generations are known as gametophytes (gamete-producing phase) and sporophytes (meiospore-producing phase). Sometimes gametophytic and sporophytic phases are identical in appearance (isomorphic), or they can look very different from each other (heteromorphic). However, there are variations on this basic pattern, and life histories of red seaweeds can be particularly complicated. Many of the specialized reproductive structures are not visible without the aid of a microscope. Because of this, seaweed reproduction is beyond the scope of this book, and we do not describe it unless it is critical for proper identification.

Table 1. Example of how increasing complexity of seaweed morphology leads to slower growth rate strategies (Murray et al. 2006).

Functional forms	Texture	Internal anatomy	Structure growth
Filamentous	soft	cells uniseriate or multiseriate	
Thin blades	soft	1-2 cell layers thick	
Coarsely branched	fleshy-wiry	cortex and medulla	Increasing complexity / Slower growth rate
Thick blades	leathery	cortex and medulla, thick cell walls	
Crustose			
fleshy	fleshy	parallel rows of cells	
coralline	stony	calcified cells	
Articulated corallines	stony	calcified, non-calcified joints	

Basic seaweed structure

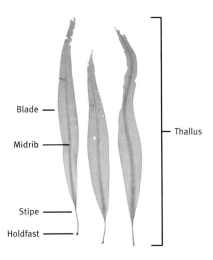

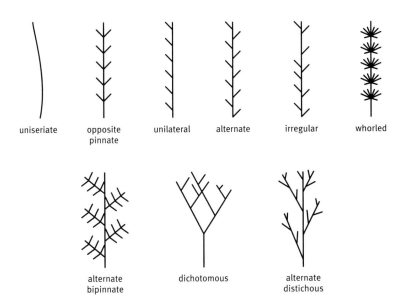

Figure 3. Diagram of common seaweed structures and branching patterns.

What are seaweeds?

Ecology

The vertical distribution of seaweeds on the shore is influenced by tidal cycles in relation to the intertidal zone—the area covered by water at high tide but exposed to air at low tide. Vertical distribution is also influenced by the substrate and wave exposure of the intertidal area.

Tidal cycles and the intertidal zone

The sun and moon's gravitational pull causes the earth's oceans to bulge and creates tides along our coastlines. Tidal cycles vary around the world. Alaska has a mixed semidiurnal tidal cycle, which results in two high and two low tides of unequal heights every day. Tidal range is the maximum vertical difference between the highest high tide and the lowest low tide, and varies in relation to coastline topography and the extent to which tidal flow is constricted. For example, the Aleutian Islands, where beaches are exposed to the open ocean, have a tidal range around 2 m (5 ft) compared to upper Cook Inlet, which has the second largest tidal range in North America, approaching 12 m (36 ft) in height.

For areas like Alaska, with mixed semidiurnal tides, the intertidal zone is the area between extreme higher high water (EHHW) and extreme lower low water (ELLW). Zero tide is mean lower low water (MLLW), and the annual average higher high tide is known as mean higher high water (MHHW). Because the tidal range varies along the coastline, the elevation of these tidal levels also varies. Of particular importance to seaweed distribution, the intertidal is commonly divided into thirds: high, mid, and low based on the average exposure of the zone to air. The area above the intertidal zone is known as the supratidal (or supralittoral), and below the intertidal is the subtidal zone (Figure 4). This scheme is commonly referred to in the habitat descriptions in this book.

Intertidal zonation and seaweed bio-bands

The dynamic nature of the intertidal zone creates many forms of stress for seaweeds. To survive, they must acquire energy from sunlight to grow, handle enormous forces from waves, tolerate variable periods exposed to air and sometimes extreme temperature changes, compete for critical habitat, defend against herbivores, and successfully reproduce. Often the result is a stratification of the seaweeds that do survive these stresses into recognizable bands or "bio-bands," which reflect their various tolerances to stress. Sometimes these bands are dominated by one seaweed or a group of closely related species. Marine invertebrates such as blue mussels and barnacles can also form bands.

Figure 4. Photo showing tidal range (26.3 ft) and major zones of the shoreline. Hesketh Island, Kachemak Bay, Alaska.

What are seaweeds?

Because seaweeds are divided into three color groups, bands are often referred to by color. Certain colors are associated with specific intertidal zones. The supratidal can have a conspicuous black band from the marine lichen *Verrucaria marina*. Rockweed is by far the most common seaweed in Alaska and forms a golden brown band in the high to mid intertidal. A green band in the mid to low intertidal often indicates disturbance where quickly growing green seaweeds thrive. A matrix of red seaweeds typically forms in the low intertidal. Understory kelps form a brown band from the low intertidal into the subtidal zone (Figure 5). The subtidal zone may have extensive beds of canopy kelps or eelgrass depending on the substrate and exposure.

Substrate and wave exposure
The type and size of the substrate in an intertidal area is the result of geological processes that include deposition rates by wind, waves, and tide. The shoreline type and orientation also determine the amount of exposure to wave energy, which can vary from a low-energy sandflat protected from wave energy by a spit or narrow bay entrance, to a high-energy beach with a bedrock substrate on an open coastline. The holdfasts of seaweeds are adapted to attach to specific types of substrates, and the seaweed as a whole is adapted to withstand a range of wave energies before being swept away.

The number of bands on a beach varies with different substrates and wave exposures. A sandy beach or small-sized substrate is difficult for seaweeds to attach to, so there is little or no banding. A cobble beach may have on average one or two bands in the mid to low intertidal depending on wave exposure. Boulders are not as mobile and tend to create wide bands that have a lot of diversity within the bands. Bedrock beaches are the most stable and show many distinct bands. The bands are usually narrower at low wave energy beaches and wider at beaches with higher energy.

Substrate is classified by size category, for example, sand, cobble, and boulder. Wave exposure is classified into the following categories: very protected (estuary), protected, semi-protected, semi-exposed, exposed, and very exposed. Because these are important influences on seaweed occurrence, we frequently refer to substrate and wave exposure classifications when describing the preferred habitat of a species (Figure 6).

Figure 5. Example of bio-bands found on a rock wall in Prince William Sound, Alaska.

What are seaweeds?

Figure 6a. Very exposed/exposed: Open coastal sites with a fetch greater than 500 km (311 mi) (distance traversed by waves without obstruction). Three distinct bio-bands are visible in this photo from Kruzof Island, Southeast Alaska: (1) a wide band of black seaside lichen in the supratidal, (2) a wide barnacle band, and (3) a wide dark brown band of kelp with patchy red seaweeds. Photo: Alaska ShoreZone.

Figure 6b. Semi-exposed: Sites subject to waves generated in distant areas or extended periods of strong local winds (maximum fetch 50-500 km, 31-311 mi). Five bio-bands are visible in this photo from Sitka Sound, Southeast Alaska: (1) a medium-width band of black seaside lichen in the supratidal, (2) barnacles with patchy red *Endocladia muricata*, (3) a wide brown band of *Alaria marginata*, (4) green surfgrass at water's edge, and (5) the offshore canopy kelp *Macrocystis pyrifera*. Photo: Alaska ShoreZone.

Figure 6c. Semi-protected: Sites subject to local winds only, waves low except during high winds (maximum fetch ~10-50 km, 6-31 mi). Five continuous bio-bands are visible in this photo from near Passage Pt., Chatham Strait, Southeast Alaska: (1) a narrow band of black seaside lichen in the supratidal, (2) brown rockweed, (3) red seaweed, (4) green seaweed, and (5) soft brown kelps in the low intertidal. Photo: Alaska ShoreZone.

Figure 6d. Protected/estuary: Sites with low waves and usually with low winds (maximum fetch 1-10 km, 0.6-6 mi). Three major bio-bands are evident in this photo from Fish Bay, Peril Strait, Chichagof Island, Southeast Alaska: (1) high band of marsh grasses and sedges, (2) patchy golden brown rockweed in the mid intertidal, and (3) a patchy band of bladed green seaweed at the water's edge. This green band is often a bed of eelgrass. Photo: Alaska ShoreZone.

Quick key

Green forms

Unbranched filaments 20

Spongy 28

Blades 34

Branched filaments 24

Tubes or sacs 30

Brown forms

Crusts 46

Finely branched 56

Branched with air bladders 66

Canopy kelps 84

Cushions or sacs 48

Coarsely branched 58

Simple bladed kelps 68

Unbranched tubes 52

Small blades 64

Sieve and ribbed kelps 76

Red forms

Fleshy Crusts 98

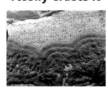

Finely branched 114

Thick blades 138

Turf forming 100

Coarsely branched 118

Blades with ribs or veins 146

Corallines 104

Thin blades 128

Other forms 152

Tubes or sacs 110

Phylum Chlorophyta

Chlorophyta, or green algae, are composed of species that occur in terrestrial, freshwater, and marine environments and display a variety of morphologies, from single-celled organisms to complex, multicellular forms. Bryophytes (mosses and others) and vascular plants arose from chlorophytan ancestors. Species in this phylum are characterized by having flagellated cells (with whiplike "tails") in which the flagella are similar in appearance. The flagella may be naked or covered with delicate hairs or scales, but they lack the tubular hairs of brown algal flagellated cells. The flagella are inserted apically. In some species, the flagellated cells are the only morphology exhibited by the species, but in green seaweeds flagellated cells occur only as reproductive cells. The chloroplast is encircled by a double membrane and contains stacked thylakoids and often one or more pyrenoids surrounded by granules of starch, the storage polysaccharide. Chloroplasts are green because the predominant photosynthetic pigments, chlorophylls *a* and *b*, are not masked by other pigments although accessory xanthophylls may be present.

Northern sea hair (*Urospora neglecta*), Sandy Cove, Akutan Island.

Common forms of green seaweeds

Unbranched filaments

Curly sea hair
  Chaetomorpha sp. 20
Green rock scum
  Rosenvingiella polyrhiza 20
Mermaid's tresses
  Ulothrix flacca 22
Northern sea hair
  Urospora neglecta 22

Branched filaments

Arctic sea moss
  Acrosiphonia arcta 24
Green rope
  Acrosiphonia coalita 24
Graceful green hair
  Cladophora sericea 26

Spongy

Sea staghorn
  Codium fragile 28
Coarse spongy cushion
  Codium ritteri 28

Tubes or sacs

Dwarf sea hair
  Blidingia minima 30
Sea hair
  Ulva intestinalis 30
Branched string lettuce
  Ulva prolifera 32
Green sea grape
  Derbesia marina 32

Blades

Emerald carpet
  Prasiola meridionalis 34
Seagrass cellophane
  Kornmannia leptoderma 34
Sea cellophane
  Monostroma grevillei 36
Dark sea lettuce
  Ulvaria obscura 36
Sea lettuce
  Ulva lactuca 38
Green string lettuce
  Ulva linza 38

Curly sea hair
Chaetomorpha sp.

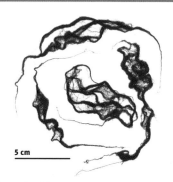

5 cm

Class Cladophorophyceae
Order Cladophorales
Family Cladophoraceae

North Pacific distribution Aleutian Islands, Alaska, to southern California; Japan; Russia.

Description Thallus is a medium to dark green, unbranched filament, with a single file of cells (uniseriate) usually occurring in tangled skeins. Cells are cylindrical (75-150 µm diameter; mostly 1-3 (occasionally to 5) times as long as wide), becoming slightly barrel-shaped when fertile. Rhizoidal branches are usually lacking.

Habitat This species often forms dense, tangled mats that float around or snag on other seaweed in the mid to low intertidal in summer. Found in protected to semi-exposed habitats, tide pools, and mudflats.

Similar to *Rhizoclonium* spp.[†] are narrower and generally prefer brackish habitats.

Green rock scum
Rosenvingiella polyrhiza
(Rosenvinge) P.C. Silva

5 cm

Former name: *Gayella polyrhiza*

Class Trebouxiophyceae
Order Prasiolales
Family Prasiolaceae

North Pacific distribution Aleutian Islands, Alaska, to Oregon.

Description Thallus is an unbranched, narrow solid cylinder (to 80 µm wide), ranging in color from light green to dark green. Mature thalli are pluriseriate and reach at least several cm in length (~1 in). They are sometimes constricted at intervals. Reproductive cells, which can contain numerous male (smaller) or female (larger) gametes, can be seen on the thallus surface.

Habitat The species is found on rock at or above high water mark and may occur mixed with species of *Prasiola. Rosenvingiella polyrhiza* can withstand long periods out of the water in protected to semi-exposed habitats. It is frequently seen as a wide band in the high intertidal of the Aleutian Islands.

Similar to *Urospora, Ulothrix.*

Curly sea hair *Chaetomorpha* sp.

Green rock scum *Rosenvingiella polyrhiza*

Mermaid's tresses
Ulothrix flacca (Dillwyn) Thuret

Former names *Conferva flacca, Ulothrix pseudoflacca*

Class Ulvophyceae
Order Ulotrichales
Family Ulotrichaceae

North Pacific distribution Arctic Ocean, Bering Sea and Aleutian Islands, Alaska, to southern California; Korea; Japan; Russia.

Description Thallus is composed of unbranched filaments with a single file of cells to 6 cm (~2.4 in) in length. The filaments usually appear coalesced and dark green on rock. The cells have a single nucleus, and although narrow (14-33 µm diameter), they are shorter (5-15 µm long) than wide. The single collar-shaped chloroplast fills the length of the cell but not the full circumference. Reproductive cells swell in the middle to 50 µm diameter.

Habitat The species forms a very slippery coating on rock in the mid to high intertidal zone in protected to semi-exposed areas in spring and early summer.

Similar to *Rosenvingiella, Urospora.*

Northern sea hair
Urospora neglecta (Kornmann) Lokhorst et Trask

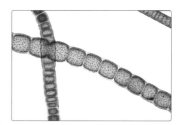

Former name *Hormiscia neglecta*

Class Ulvophyceae
Order Ulotrichales
Family Ulotrichaceae

North Pacific distribution Arctic Ocean, Bering Sea and Aleutian Islands, Alaska, to Washington.

Description Thallus is an unbranched filament with a single file of cells (uniseriate) that can reach at least 3.0 cm (1.2 in) in length. The multinucleate cells of the filament are squat, quadrate, or barrel-shaped, 13-70 µm diameter (average 40 µm) and 18-50 µm long (average 31 µm) and have a reticulate chloroplast. The holdfast has relatively few (<5) rhizoids.

Habitat The species is found on bedrock, boulder, and cobble in the mid to high intertidal zone in spring and early summer in semi-protected to semi-exposed habitats.

Similar to *Rosenvingiella, Ulothrix.*

Mermaid's tresses *Ulothrix flacca*

Northern sea hair *Urospora neglecta*

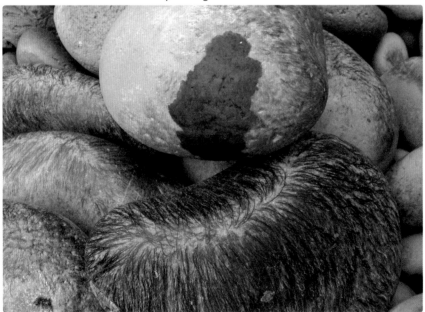

Green Seaweeds

Arctic sea moss
Acrosiphonia arcta (Dillwyn) Gain

Former names *Conferva arcta,
Cladophora arcta, Spongomorpha arcta*

Class Ulvophyceae
Order Ulotrichales
Family Ulotrichaceae

North Pacific distribution Arctic Ocean,
Bering Sea and Aleutian Islands, Alaska,
to Oregon; Russia.

2 cm

Description The dark green thallus forms distinctive mats or tufts up to 6 cm (2.25 in) tall. Uniseriate filaments branch from sides of cells, and branches are held together by colorless rhizoids (curved branches are rare). The tips of the branches are usually rounded and at least as broad as lower portions. Cells are longer than broad. Seaweeds in this genus wring out like a sponge when squeezed, drying out the thallus.

Habitat The species occurs on boulders and bedrock in the mid to low intertidal of protected to semi-exposed habitats in spring and summer.

Similar to *Acrosiphonia coalita, A. duriuscula*, Cladophora sericea.*

Green rope
Acrosiphonia coalita (Ruprecht) Scagel,
Garbary, Golden et M.W. Hawkes

Former names *Acrosiphonia mertensii,
Spongomorpha coalita*

Class Ulvophyceae
Order Ulotrichales
Family Ulotrichaceae

North Pacific distribution Northern Gulf of
Alaska to central California.

2 cm

Description The green thallus forms 10-20 cm (4-8 in) tall rope-like strands from branched, uniseriate filaments. Branching is lateral, from sides of cells, and cells are longer than broad. The frayed rope appearance is caused by hook-shaped branches that entangle neighboring branches to form rope-like strands.

Habitat The species is found on rock in the mid to low intertidal in protected to semi-exposed habitats in spring and early summer.

Similar to *Acrosiphonia arcta, A. duriuscula*.*

Arctic sea moss *Acrosiphonia arcta*

Green rope *Acrosiphonia coalita*

Graceful green hair
Cladophora sericea (Hudson) Kützing

Former names *Conferva sericea,*
Cladophora glaucescens

Class Cladophorophyceae
Order Cladophorales
Family Cladophoraceae

North Pacific distribution Aleutian Islands,
Alaska, to San Diego, California; Korea; Japan.

5 cm

Description Thallus is green to light green and made of delicately branched, uniseriate filaments 5-20 cm (2-8 in) tall. Branching is from ends of cells, and branches become narrower toward their tips. The thallus frequently forms extensive mats in undisturbed areas.

Habitat This species is very common and is found on all substrates, forming mats in the mid to low intertidal in predominantly protected areas and in high intertidal pools at more exposed sites.

Similar to *Ulva prolifera, Acrosiphonia arcta.*

Graceful green hair *Cladophora sericea*

Cladophora bio-band in Prince William Sound, Alaska

Green Seaweeds

Sea staghorn

Codium fragile (Suringar) Hariot subsp.
californicum (J. Agardh) Maggs et J. Kelly

Former name *Codium mucronatum*
f. *californicum*

Class Bryopsidophyceae
Order Bryopsidales
Family Codiaceae

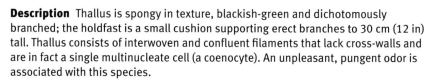

5 cm

North Pacific distribution Green Island, Prince
William Sound, Alaska, to Baja California, Mexico.

Description Thallus is spongy in texture, blackish-green and dichotomously branched; the holdfast is a small cushion supporting erect branches to 30 cm (12 in) tall. Thallus consists of interwoven and confluent filaments that lack cross-walls and are in fact a single multinucleate cell (a coenocyte). An unpleasant, pungent odor is associated with this species.

Habitat The species is typically found on bedrock or boulders in the low intertidal of semi-exposed coasts.

Coarse spongy cushion

Codium ritteri Setchell et N.L. Gardner

Class Bryopsidophyceae
Order Bryopsidales
Family Codiaceae

North Pacific distribution Bering Sea and
Aleutian Islands, Alaska, to northern British
Columbia; Russia.

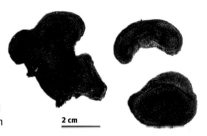

2 cm

Description Thallus is coarse, green spongy cushions up to 4 cm (1.5 in) tall and 10 cm (4 in) in diameter. The minute dots visible to the naked eye on the surface of the cushions are the tips of swollen filaments, a distinction from *Codium setchellii*.

Habitat *Codium ritteri* is found in semi-exposed to semi-protected areas on bedrock or large boulders in the low intertidal and subtidal to depths of 24 m (79 ft).

Similar to *Codium setchellii**.

Sea staghorn *Codium fragile*

Coarse spongy cushion *Codium ritteri*

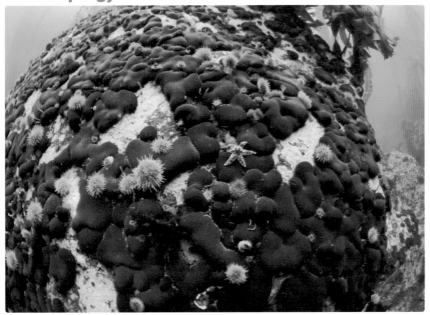

Green Seaweeds

Dwarf sea hair
Blidingia minima (Nägeli ex Kützing) Kylin var. *minima*

Former names *Enteromorpha minima*, *E. nana*

Class Ulvophyceae
Order Ulvales
Family Kornmanniaceae

North Pacific distribution Arctic Ocean, Bering Sea and Aleutian Islands, Alaska, to Mexico; China; Korea; Japan; Russia.

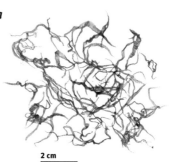

2 cm

Description Thalli grow as clusters of light green, cylindrical to flattened hollow tubes, often wrinkled or twisted, arising from a discoidal cushion. This species usually does not exceed 5-10 cm (2-4 in) tall so is usually shorter than *Ulva intestinalis*, and cells are smaller (≤5-7 μm diameter) than those of *U. intestinalis*.

Habitat *Blidingia minima* is found growing on cobble, boulders, bedrock, barnacles, driftwood, and even other algae throughout the intertidal in semi-protected and protected habitats, especially if recently disturbed.

Similar to *Pseudothrix borealis**, *Ulva intestinalis*.

Sea hair
Ulva intestinalis Linnaeus

Former name *Enteromorpha intestinalis*

Class Ulvophyceae
Order Ulvales
Family Ulvaceae

North Pacific distribution Arctic Ocean, Bering Sea and Aleutian Islands, Alaska, to Mexico; Korea; Japan; Russia.

5 cm

Description The bright to pale green tubular thallus is 20 cm (8 in) or more tall and up to 5 mm (0.2 in) in width. The hollow tubes can be constricted at irregular intervals like intestines. Cells are >10 μm diameter.

Habitat This species thrives in high intertidal seepage areas or tide pools, attached or free-floating. It is frequently found in protected habitats or areas influenced by freshwater.

Similar to *Blidingia minima*, *Pseudothrix borealis**, *Ulva linza*.

Dwarf sea hair *Blidingia minima var. minima*

Sea hair *Ulva intestinalis*

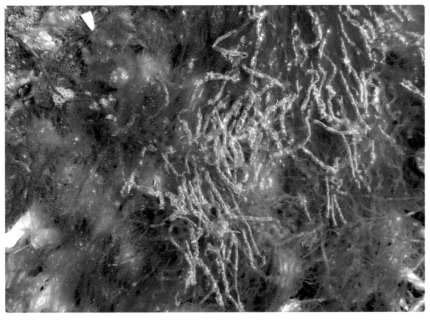

Green Seaweeds

Branched string lettuce
Ulva prolifera O.F. Müller

Former name *Enteromorpha prolifera*

Class Ulvophyceae

Order Ulvales

Family Ulvaceae

North Pacific distribution Arctic Ocean, Bering Sea and Aleutian Islands, Alaska, to Mexico; China; Korea; Japan; Russia.

5 cm

Description Thallus is tubular, although it can appear filamentous because of its narrow diameter. Few to many branches proliferate from the tube. It forms extensive mats several meters (many feet) in length. The color can range from green to very light green.

Habitat The species is found on protected beaches attached to cobble or smaller substrates, or free-floating in muddy areas in summer.

Similar to *Cladophora sericea.*

Green sea grape
Derbesia marina (Lyngbye) Solier (Halicystis phase)

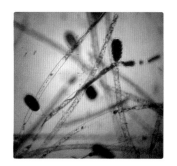

Former names *Halicystis ovalis, Derbesia pacifica*

Class Bryopsidophyceae

Order Bryopsidales

Family Derbesiaceae

North Pacific distribution Aleutian Islands, Alaska, to Baja California, Mexico; Korea; Japan; Russia.

Description Thallus is a hollow, spherical ball with a short stalk; it is the gametophytic phase in the life cycle of the species. It usually grows to 10 mm (0.4 in) tall, and within the sphere are many peripherally located chloroplasts and nuclei. The sporophytic *Derbesia* phase forms branching, filamentous tufts only 1 cm (<½ in) tall.

Habitat This species prefers growing on encrusting coralline algae on semi-exposed coasts in the very low intertidal to subtidal.

Branched string lettuce *Ulva prolifera*

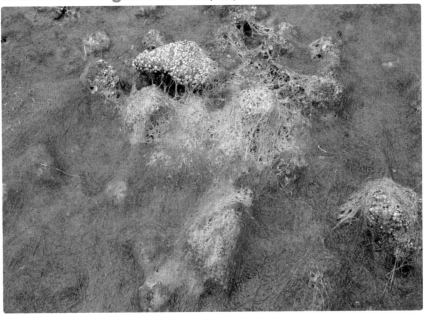

Green sea grape *Derbesia marina*

Green Seaweeds

Emerald carpet
Prasiola meridionalis Setchell et N.L. Gardner

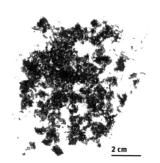

Class Trebouxiophyceae

Order Prasiolales

Family Prasiolaceae

North Pacific distribution Aleutian Islands, Alaska, to California.

2 cm

Description Thalli of this species form a carpet of many tiny (up to 8 mm or 0.3 in tall), green, undivided blades. The blades have short stalks basally and are often curved and hoodlike at their tips. Cells are quadrate or rectangular, 5-9 μm long and wide, and not clustered in groups of four or more with spaces between groups of cells.

Habitat The species is found on rock in the high intertidal to above high water mark. It is frequently associated with bird rookeries where guano provides high concentrations of nitrogenous compounds that it tolerates or needs.

Similar to Prasiola borealis*.

Seagrass cellophane
Kornmannia leptoderma (Kjellman) Bliding

Former names Kornmannia zostericola, Monostroma zostericola

Class Ulvophyceae

Order Ulvales

Family Kornmanniaceae

North Pacific distribution Alaska Peninsula, Alaska, to San Luis Obispo County, California; Japan; Russia.

2 cm

Description Thallus is a thin, bright green blade up to 8 cm (3 in) tall with finely ruffled margins. Blades, which are one cell thick, start out as small sacs, then split open as they expand. Cells are small, 4-6 μm diameter.

Habitat This annual grows only on seagrass from semi-exposed to protected habitats.

Similar to Monostroma.

Emerald carpet *Prasiola meridionalis*

Seagrass cellophane *Kornmannia leptoderma*

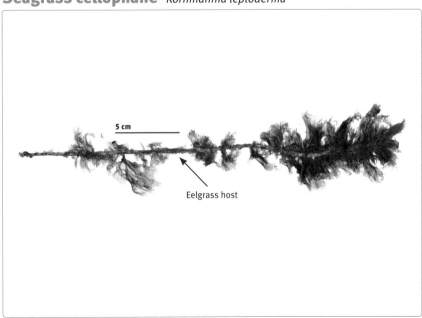

5 cm

Eelgrass host

Sea cellophane
Monostroma grevillei (Thuret) Wittrock

2 cm

Former names *Enteromorpha grevillei, Monostroma arcticum*

Class Ulvophyceae
Order Ulotrichales
Family Gomontiaceae

North Pacific distribution Bering Sea and Aleutian Islands, Alaska, to Monterey County, California; Korea; Japan; Russia.

Description A young thallus starts out as a sac and as it matures it splits and forms a blade to 30 cm (12 in) tall, although usually much smaller. The delicate, light green, transparent blade is a single layer of cells only 30 μm thick. Cells are ~16 μm diameter.

Habitat The species occurs in the spring on protected and semi-protected coasts and can grow epiphytically on other seaweeds such as *Fucus*.

Similar to *Kornmannia, Ulva, Ulvaria.*

Dark sea lettuce
Ulvaria obscura (Kützing) Gayral **var. *blyttii*** (Areschoug) Bliding

5 cm

Former names *Monostroma fuscum, Ulvaria fusca, Ulvaria splendens, Ulva blyttii*

Class Ulvophyceae
Order Ulvales
Family Ulvaceae

North Pacific distribution Bering Sea and Aleutian Islands, Alaska, to northern Washington; Korea; Japan; Russia.

Description A young thallus starts out as a sac and then splits into a blade expanding to at least 30 cm (12 in) in diameter. The blade is bright green, one cell layer thick (up to 72 μm), and almost opaque. When dried, the thallus can turn dark brown to almost black due to the presence of dopamine in cells.

Habitat The species is found in the low intertidal and subtidal on protected and semi-protected coasts and is frequently found on pebble or cobble substrates.

Similar to *Monostroma, Ulva.*

Sea cellophane *Monostroma grevillei*

Dark sea lettuce *Ulvaria obscura* var. *blyttii*

Sea lettuce
Ulva lactuca Linnaeus

2 cm

Former name *Ulva fenestrata*

Class Ulvophyceae
Order Ulvales
Family Ulvaceae

North Pacific distribution Arctic coast of Alaska
to California; China; Korea; Japan; Russia.

Description Thallus is a green blade consisting of two cell layers, commonly with numerous small holes or perforations scattered throughout, reaching 60 cm (24 in) or more tall, although frequently much smaller. Cells are 10-20 μm in diameter, and the blade can be 70 μm thick (significantly thicker than *Monostroma*).

Habitat *Ulva lactuca* occurs in the mid to low intertidal on cobble, boulders, and bedrock. It prefers protected and semi-protected habitats.

Similar to *Monostroma, Ulvaria.*

Green string lettuce
Ulva linza Linnaeus

5 cm

Former name *Enteromorpha linza*

Class Ulvophyceae
Order Ulvales
Family Ulvaceae

North Pacific distribution Arctic Ocean, Bering
Sea and Aleutian Islands, Alaska, to Mexico;
Taiwan; Korea; Japan; Russia.

Description There is no doubt recognizing this distinctive species. The bright green thallus is tubular at the base but flattened above. It grows into long, narrow, ruffled blades two cell layers thick, 1-4 cm (0.4-1.6 in) wide and up to 45 cm tall. Cells are 10-15 μm diameter.

Habitat The species is found in the mid to low intertidal on cobble, boulders, and bedrock. It prefers protected and semi-protected habitats.

Similar to *Ulva californica*[†], *U. intestinalis.*

Sea lettuce *Ulva lactuca*

Green string lettuce *Ulva linza*

Green Seaweeds

Northern green rope
Acrosiphonia duriuscula (Ruprecht) Yendo

> **North Pacific distribution** Aleutian Islands to Southeast Alaska; Japan; Russia.

Description Thallus is green, growing in tufts 2-15 cm (1-6 in) tall, composed of branched, interwoven, uniseriate filaments with simple, sparse, hooklike branchlets. Cells are often shorter than broad. The overall aspect is usually spreading, but the species occasionally forms dense, ropelike tangles. The species is an annual found on rock in the low intertidal of semi-protected to semi-exposed habitats.

Coarse green sea hair
Chaetomorpha melagonium
(F. Weber et Mohr) Kützing

> **North Pacific distribution** Arctic Ocean, Bering Sea, and Aleutian Islands, Alaska, to Oregon; Japan; Russia.

Description Thallus is a dark green unbranched, uniseriate filament, which is fairly smooth and rigid and grows in clusters. The cells of each filament are large enough to see with the naked eye. This perennial occurs on rock or as unattached strands in the low intertidal and subtidal of protected to semi-exposed habitats.

Smooth spongy cushion
Codium setchellii N.L. Gardner

> **North Pacific distribution** Northern Southeast Alaska (Chichagof Island) to Baja California, Mexico.

Description Thallus is a dark green spongy cushion 25 cm (10 in) or more in diameter and 15 mm (0.6 in) or less thick. Because the filaments of the thallus are narrow, the tips are not visible to the naked eye, and the surface appears smooth. This perennial occurs on rock in the very low intertidal or shallow subtidal of semi-exposed and exposed habitats.

Northern emerald carpet
Prasiola borealis M. Reed

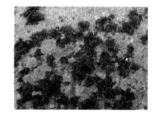

> **North Pacific distribution** Aleutian Islands, Alaska, to British Columbia; Commander Islands, Russia.

Description Thallus is a small (up to 10 mm or 0.4 in tall), dark olive green blade, which is infected by the fungus *Guignardia alaskana* M. Reed. The blades have short stalks basally, are broader than tall, often with curled edges. Cells are clustered in groups of four or more with spaces between groups of cells The species forms extensive carpets on supratidal bedrock of protected to exposed shores.

Jade necklace
Urospora wormskioldii (Mertens ex Hornemann) Rosenvinge

North Pacific distribution Aleutian Islands, Alaska, to San Luis Obispo County, California; Japan; Russia.

Description Thallus is a dark green, unbranched, uniseriate filament. When fertile, the single chain of barrel-shaped cells, visible to the naked eye, looks like a necklace of small jade beads. This spring ephemeral is found on rock (usually cobble) in the low intertidal of semi-exposed habitats.

False northern thread
Pseudothrix borealis Hanic et S.C. Lindstrom

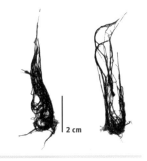

North Pacific distribution Bering Sea and Aleutian Islands to Cook Inlet, Alaska; Japan; Russia.

Description Thallus is an emerald green tube to 10 cm tall and very narrow (~1 mm diameter). Cells are small (3-6 μm diameter), rounded, often in groups of 2 or 4 basally, larger (~15 μm diameter) at distal end of thallus. The species is found on mid to lower intertidal boulders and bedrock in spring and early summer.

2 cm

Green bio-band of *Urospora neglecta*, Unalaska Island, Aleutian Islands.

Brown Seaweeds

Phylum Ochrophyta

All brown algae are multicellular and belong to the class Phaeophyceae, phylum Ochrophyta. The phylum and class names come from the color of this distinctive group of seaweeds. Almost all brown algal species are marine, and the largest and most morphologically complex marine algae are brown algae.

Brown algae are also distinguished by the two different types of flagella borne by the swimming reproductive cells. The forward directed flagellum bears stiff tubular hairs called mastigonemes and is usually longer than the smooth, backward-directed flagellum. The only flagellated cells are reproductive cells (there are no free-living flagellated unicells in the class Phaeophyceae), and the flagella are inserted laterally or subapically.

Brown algal chloroplasts are usually golden brown in color because of the accessory pigment fucoxanthin. Cell walls are composed of a fibrillar cellulose network and an alginate mucilage. The chloroplast is surrounded by four membranes: the double membrane of the chloroplast envelope, and the chloroplast endoplasmic reticulum, which is often continuous with the nuclear envelope. Thylakoids within the chloroplast are stacked in groups of three, and the primary pigments are chlorophylls a, c_1, and c_2. The main storage product of photosynthesis is laminarin, a β-1,3-linked polymer of glucose; it is stored outside the chloroplast.

Laminarian kelps in the sun, Seldovia Point, Seldovia.

Common forms of brown seaweeds

Crusts

Sea fungus
  Ralfsia fungiformis 46
Brown spot
  Ralfsia phase 46

Cushions or sacs

Sea chip
  Coilodesme bulligera 48
Sea rubber
  Colpomenia bullosa 48
Sea cauliflower
  Leathesia marina 50
Studded sea balloons
  Soranthera ulvoidea 50

Unbranched tubes

Twisted sea tubes
  Melanosiphon intestinalis 52
Soda straws
  Scytosiphon lomentaria 52
Golden bottlebrush epiphyte
  Saundersella simplex 54
Spaghetti kelp
  Chorda filum 54

Common forms of brown seaweeds

Finely branched

Sea felt
Pylaiella littoralis 56
False sea felt
Ectocarpus siliculosus 57
Brown sea moss
Sphacelaria rigidula 57

Coarsely branched

Bottlebrush seaweed
Analipus japonicus 58
Chocolate pencils
Chordaria flagelliformis 58
Witch's hair
Desmarestia aculeata 60
Stringy acid kelp
Desmarestia viridis 60
Golden sea hair
Dictyosiphon foeniculaceus 62
Gooey golden seaweed
Eudesme virescens 63
Anderson's gooey brown
Haplogloia andersonii 63

Small blades

False kelp
Petalonia fascia 64
Eelgrass brown blade
Punctaria lobata 64

Branched with air bladders

Northern bladder chain
Stephanocystis geminata 66
Rockweed or popweed
Fucus distichus 66

Common forms of kelps

Simple bladed kelps

Golden V kelp
Aureophycus aleuticus[1] 68
Northern rhizome kelp
Laminaria longipes 68
Southern stiff-stiped kelp
Laminaria setchellii 70
Arctic suction-cup kelp
Laminaria solidungula 70
Suction-cup kelp
Laminaria yezoensis 72
Sugar kelp
Saccharina latissima 72
Sea cabbage
Saccharina sessilis 74
Split kelp
Saccharina groenlandica 74

Sieve and ribbed kelps

Spiral sieve kelp
Agarum clathrus 76
Sieve kelp
Agarum clathratum 78
Ribbon kelp
Alaria marginata 78
Five-ribbed kelp
Costaria costata 80
Three-ribbed kelp
Cymathaere triplicata 80
Flat pompom kelp
Lessoniopsis littoralis 82
Broad-ribbed kelp
Pleurophycus gardneri 82

Canopy kelps

Dragon kelp
Eualaria fistulosa 84
Giant kelp
Macrocystis pyrifera 86
Bull kelp
Nereocystis luetkeana 88

---

[1]species found only in Alaska

Sea fungus

Ralfsia fungiformis (Gunnerus) Setchell et N.L. Gardner

2 cm

Former names *Fucus fungiformis*, *Ralfsia deusta*

Class Phaeophyceae
Order Ralfsiales
Family Ralfsiaceace

North Pacific distribution Arctic Ocean, Bering Sea and Aleutian Islands, Alaska, to Humboldt County, California; Korea; Japan; Russia.

Description The thallus of this species resembles a fungus, with broadly overlapping lobes that are olive brown to yellowish at the edges and free of the substrate. Thalli form nearly circular patches 1 mm thick and 2-6 cm (0.8-2.4 in) in diameter. This slow growing perennial has concentric growth lines visible on the lobes.

Habitat This species is found on rock in the mid to low intertidal, including tide pools, and prefers protected to semi-exposed habitats.

Similar to *Ralfsia* spp.

Brown spot
Ralfsia phase

5 cm

Former name *Ralfsia californica*

Class Phaeophyceae
Order Ectocarpales
Family Scytosiphonaceae

North Pacific distribution Arctic Ocean, Bering Sea and Aleutian Islands, Alaska, to Baja California, Mexico; China; Korea; Japan; Russia.

Description Thallus forms a thin (mostly <100 μm), smooth brown crust, which is firmly attached to substrate. Crusts are small (<5 mm diameter) and circular or larger and confluent. Some crusts have erect brown algae *Petalonia fascia* or *Scytosiphon lomentaria* growing out of them, suggesting they are the alternate sporophytic phase or the basal system of those species.

Habitat This crust occurs in high to mid intertidal pools and on low intertidal rock of semi-exposed to semi-protected habitats.

Similar to *Ralfsia fungiformis*.

Sea fungus *Ralfsia fungiformis*

Brown spot *Ralfsia phase*

Sea chip
Coilodesme bulligera Strömfelt

5 cm

Class Phaeophyceae

Order Ectocarpales

Family Chordariaceae

North Pacific distribution Aleutian Islands, Alaska, to Cape Arago, Oregon; Commander Islands, Russia.

Description Thallus is a thin-walled, tan-colored sac that is flattened and tapers to a short stipe and inconspicuous disc-like (discoidal) holdfast. The thallus averages 15 cm (5.9 in) but has been observed in Alaska up to 50 cm (20 in) tall.

Habitat This annual occurs in spring, usually on mid to low intertidal cobble or pebble in areas that remain damp at low tide in protected habitats. This species is not epiphytic on other seaweeds.

Similar to *Colpomenia bullosa, Petalonia, Coilodesme* sp.[†]

Sea rubber
Colpomenia bullosa (D.A. Saunders) Yamada

5 cm

Former name *Scytosiphon bullosus*

Class Phaeophyceae

Order Ectocarpales

Family Scytosiphonaceae

North Pacific distribution Unalaska Island, Alaska, to central California; China; Korea, Japan.

Description Thallus is a cylindrical, yellowish-brown sac with a contorted cushion-like base and holdfast. Thallus generally doesn't grow larger than 20 cm (7.9 in) tall.

Habitat This annual is found in the low intertidal zone growing on rock and prefers semi-protected to semi-exposed habitats.

Similar to *Coilodesme bulligera, Leathesia.*

Sea chip *Coilodesme bulligera*

Sea rubber *Colpomenia bullosa*

Sea cauliflower

Leathesia marina (Lyngbye) Decaisne

Former names *Chaetophora marina*, *Tremella difformis*, *Leathesia difformis*

Class Phaeophyceae

Order Ectocarpales

Family Chordariaceae

North Pacific distribution Unalaska Island, Alaska, to Baja California, Mexico; China; Korea; Japan; Russia.

2 cm

Description Thallus forms distinctive yellowish-brown, hollow globular cushions that are deeply convoluted. The individual fleshy thalli are 1-6 cm (0.4-2.4 in) across but may become larger as they grow into each other and form a bubbly carpet.

Habitat This annual species can be found on rock or as an epiphyte on other seaweeds in the high to low intertidal from protected to semi-exposed habitats.

Similar to young *Soranthera*, *Colpomenia bullosa*, *C. peregrina**.

Studded sea balloons

Soranthera ulvoidea Postels et Ruprecht

Class Phaeophyceae

Order Ectocarpales

Family Chordariaceae

North Pacific distribution Bering Sea and Aleutian Islands, Alaska, to Santa Barbara, California; Commander Islands, Russia.

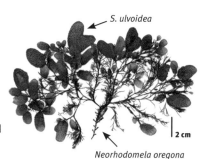

S. ulvoidea

2 cm

Neorhodomela oregona

Description Thallus is a pale to olive brown sac with dark brown bumps, tapering to an inconspicuous, discoidal holdfast. The thallus is 1-5 cm (0.4-2 in) tall and is strictly an epiphyte on species of *Neorhodomela* and *Odonthalia*.

Habitat This summer annual is found in the mid to low intertidal from protected to semi-exposed habitats.

Similar to young *Leathesia*.

Sea cauliflower *Leathesia marina*

Studded sea balloons *Soranthera ulvoidea*

Brown Seaweeds

Twisted sea tubes
Melanosiphon intestinalis
(D.A. Saunders) M.J. Wynne

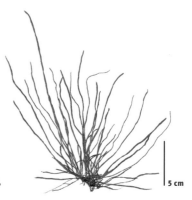

Former name *Myelophycus intestinalis*

Class Phaeophyceae
Order Ectocarpales
Family Chordariaceae

North Pacific distribution Bering Sea and Aleutian Islands, Alaska, to San Mateo County, California; Korea; Japan.

5 cm

Description Thallus is a partly hollow, unbranched cylinder lacking constrictions and ranging from light to dark brown in color, usually with a reddish cast, and sometimes appearing twisted. Clusters of the tubular thalli arise from a discoidal holdfast and often form mats. Thalli grow up to 35 cm (13.7 in) tall.

Habitat This weedy annual can be found in high tide pools and on mid to low intertidal rock from protected to semi-exposed habitats.

Similar to *Scytosiphon* spp.

Soda straws
Scytosiphon lomentaria (Lyngbye) Link

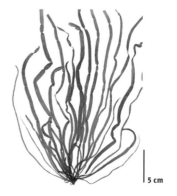

Former names *Scytosiphon simplicissimus*, *Chorda lomentaria*

Class Phaeophyceae
Order Ectocarpales
Family Scytosiphonaceae

North Pacific distribution Bering Sea and Aleutian Islands, Alaska, to Baja California, Mexico; China; Korea; Japan; Russia.

5 cm

Description Thallus is a conspicuous golden brown, unbranched tube with constrictions at more or less regular intervals. Thalli range from 20 to 50 cm (8-20 in) tall and are ~1 cm (0.4 in) wide; some Alaska specimens reach over 75 cm (29.5 in) tall. Thalli grow in clusters from a discoidal *Ralfsia*-like holdfast.

Habitat This weedy annual is commonly found on rock in the mid to low intertidal and in tide pools, and ranges from protected to semi-exposed habitats.

Similar to *Melanosiphon*, *Scytosiphon* spp.[†], *Chorda filum*.

Twisted sea tubes *Melanosiphon intestinalis*

Soda straws *Scytosiphon lomentaria*

Brown Seaweeds

Golden bottlebrush epiphyte
Saundersella simplex (D.A. Saunders) Kylin

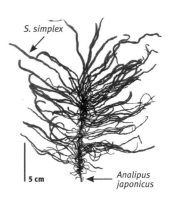

S. simplex

Former names *Gobia simplex, Mesogloia simplex*

Class Phaeophyceae

Order Ectocarpales

Family Chordariaceae

North Pacific distribution Alaska Peninsula, Alaska, to southern British Columbia; Japan.

5 cm

Analipus japonicus

Description The tubular and mucilaginous unbranched thallus is strictly epiphytic on *Analipus japonicus*. The golden brown thallus of *Saundersella simplex* frequently dominates its host, growing up to 18 cm (7 in) long.

Habitat This summer annual is found on its host in the mid to low intertidal of semi-protected to exposed habitats.

Similar to *Melanosiphon, Scytosiphon*.

Spaghetti kelp
Chorda filum (Linnaeus) Stackhouse

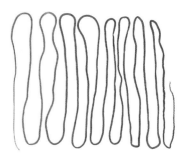

Former names *Fucus filum, Chordaria filum, Scytosiphon filum, Chondrus filum*

Class Phaeophyceae

Order Laminariales

Family Chordaceae

North Pacific distribution Arctic Ocean and Bering Sea to Prince William Sound, Alaska; northern Washington; China; Korea; Japan; Russia.

Description This light brown kelp has a long, firm, smooth, cylindrical whiplike thallus 0.5 cm (0.2 in) in diameter and up to 1 m (3.3 ft) or more tall, which tapers to a tiny discoidal holdfast. Air pockets are visible inside the thallus, causing the thallus to float toward the surface. There are no constrictions along the thallus.

Habitat This uncommon kelp is an annual and may be found growing on rock (often pebble or cobble) in the very low intertidal to upper subtidal in protected habitats with slight current.

Similar to *Scytosiphon lomentaria, Halosiphon tomentosus*[†].

Golden bottlebrush epiphyte *Saundersella simplex*

Spaghetti kelp *Chorda filum*

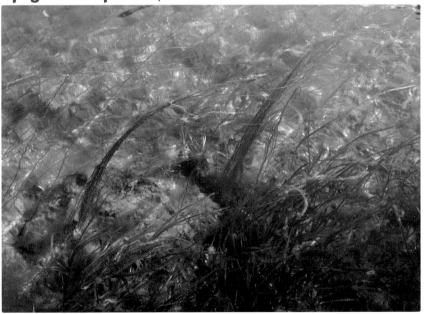

Sea felt
Pylaiella littoralis (Linnaeus) Kjellman

Former names *Pilayella littoralis*, *Conferva littoralis*

Class Phaeophyceae

Order Ectocarpales

Family Acinetosporaceae

P. littoralis

2 cm   Rockweed

North Pacific distribution Arctic Ocean, Bering Sea and Aleutian Islands, Alaska, to southern California; Korea; Japan; Russia.

Description Thallus is yellowish to dark brown, composed of uniseriate filaments to 60 μm diameter, richly branched in an opposite, rarely alternate pattern (visible microscopically). Cells bearing opposite branches are often trapezoidal in shape. Reproductive cells are intercalary (not terminal) on branches. This species commonly grows on rockweed and blooms into large mats, covering its host.

Habitat This ephemeral species is found on rock, other algae, or free floating in the mid intertidal of protected and estuarine habitats.

Similar to *Ectocarpus*, *Elachista**, *Sphacelaria*.

Sea felt *Pylaiella littoralis*

False sea felt

Ectocarpus siliculosus (Dillwyn) Lyngbye

Former name *Conferva siliculosa*

Class Phaeophyceae
Order Ectocarpales
Family Ectocarpaceae

North Pacific distribution Arctic coast of Alaska
south to central California; Korea; Japan.

host: *Scytosiphon lomentaria*

Description Thallus is light brown, with very finely branched uniseriate filaments to
60 μm diameter and reaching at least 8 cm (3 in) tall. Branches taper and are more or
less alternate. The cells have several ribbonlike chloroplasts per cell.

Habitat The species is usually epiphytic on other algae in low intertidal sheltered
habitats in mid to late summer.

Similar to *Elachista*, Pylaiella, Sphacelaria.*

Brown sea moss

Sphacelaria rigidula Kützing

Former names *Sphacelaria furcigera,
S. subfusca*

Class Phaeophyceae
Order Sphacelariales
Family Sphacelariaceae

North Pacific distribution Alaska Peninsula,
Alaska, to Mexico; China, Japan.

Description Thallus is composed of fine, brown filaments, which grow in small tufts
to about 1 cm (0.4 in) tall from basal rhizoids. Branching is irregular and only visible
under a microscope. The elongate apical cell is the same width as the rest of the
filament, which can become polysiphonous.

Habitat This often-overlooked perennial occurs on rock from the high to low
intertidal of protected to semi-exposed habitats.

Similar to *Ectocarpus, Elachista*, Pylaiella.*

57

Bottlebrush seaweed

Analipus japonicus (Harvey) M.J. Wynne

Former names *Halosaccion japonicum, Heterochordaria abietina, Chordaria abietina*

Class Phaeophyceae

Order Ralfsiales

Family Ralfsiaceae

North Pacific distribution Aleutian Islands, Alaska, to Point Conception, California; Korea; Japan; Russia.

Description Thallus is light to dark brown with numerous radially arranged flattened lateral branches, which are somewhat curled at the ends and hollow. This species has a distinctive perennial crustose base up to 5 cm (2 in) in diameter, and erect axes up to 35 cm (14 in) tall that die back in the fall.

Habitat This species occurs in the mid to low intertidal on rock and prefers semi-protected to exposed habitats. The epiphyte *Saundersella simplex* is frequently attached to the central axis and can nearly obscure its host.

Chocolate pencils

Chordaria flagelliformis (O.F. Müller) C. Agardh

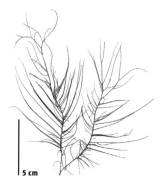

Former name *Fucus flagelliformis*

Class Phaeophyceae

Order Ectocarpales

Family Chordariaceae

North Pacific distribution Arctic Ocean and Bering Sea to Southeast Alaska; Korea; Japan; Russia.

Description Thallus is light to dark brown; it averages 30 cm (12 in) but can reach 50 cm (20 in) tall. The long, sparse branches are slender like the main axis, smooth, and quite firm; they are arranged irregularly and rarely branch themselves.

Habitat This annual is found on rock in the low intertidal, including tide pools, and prefers protected to semi-exposed habitats. *Dictyosiphon foeniculaceus* is a common epiphyte.

Similar to *Desmarestia, Dictyosiphon*.

Bottlebrush seaweed *Analipus japonicus*

Perennial crustose base

Chocolate pencils *Chordaria flagelliformis*

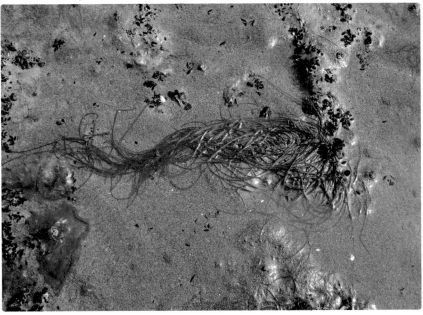

Brown Seaweeds

Witch's hair
Desmarestia aculeata (Linnaeus) J.V. Lamouroux

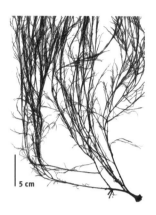

5 cm

Former names *Fucus aculeatus,
Desmarestia intermedia*

Class Phaeophyceae
Order Desmarestiales
Family Desmarestiaceae

North Pacific distribution Arctic Ocean, Bering
Sea and Aleutian Islands, Alaska, to northern
Washington; Russia.

Description The medium brown to almost black thallus is coarse, with cylindrical to
slightly flattened branches arranged in an alternate pattern and a discoidal holdfast.
The main axis is stiff and up to 5 mm (0.2 in) wide, and the whole individual can be
up to 2 m (6.5 ft) tall.

Habitat This perennial is found on rock (including cobble) in the low intertidal to
subtidal zones from protected to semi-exposed habitats.

Similar to *Chordaria*.

Stringy acid kelp
Desmarestia viridis (O.F. Müller) J.V. Lamouroux

5 cm

Former names *Fucus viridis,
Desmarestia media* var. *tenuis*

Class Phaeophyceae
Order Desmarestiales
Family Desmarestiaceae

North Pacific distribution Arctic Ocean,
Bering Sea and Aleutian Islands, Alaska to Baja
California, Mexico; China; Korea; Japan; Russia.

Description The light brown thallus has a cylindrical central axis, opposite
branching, and a discoidal holdfast. The thallus is often delicate. It grows up to 120
cm (48 in) tall and is considered the most acidic of all the acid kelps, destroying itself
and other seaweeds when damaged, by releasing sulfuric acid.

Habitat This perennial is found on rock in the very low intertidal to subtidal zones in
semi-protected to exposed habitats.

Similar to *Chordaria, Dictyosiphon*.

Witch's hair *Desmarestia aculeata*

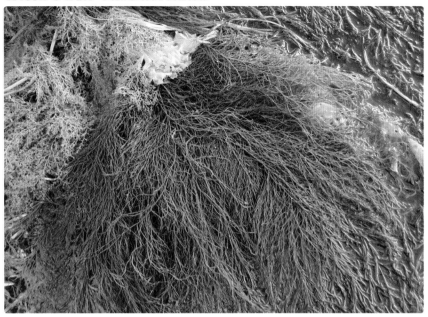

Stringy acid kelp *Desmarestia viridis*

Golden sea hair

Dictyosiphon foeniculaceus (Hudson) Greville

5 cm

Former name *Conferva foeniculacea*

Class Phaeophyceae

Order Ectocarpales

Family Chordariaceae

North Pacific distribution Arctic Ocean, Bering Sea and Aleutian Islands, Alaska, to northern Washington; Japan; Russia.

Description Thallus is golden brown with multiple orders of branches, which are delicate, progressively narrower, and alternate, opposite, or irregular. Thallus is very fine and reaches 20-40 cm (7-16 in) tall.

Habitat This annual grows epiphytically on other seaweeds, attached to rock, or forms free-floating mats in protected and estuarine habitats. The seaweeds *Chordaria flagelliformis* and *Scytosiphon lomentaria* are common hosts for this species.

Similar to *Dictyosiphon*, *Desmarestia*.

Golden sea hair *Dictyosiphon foeniculaceus*

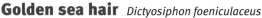

Gooey golden seaweed
Eudesme virescens (Carmichael ex Berkeley) J. Agardh

2 cm

Former names *Mesogloia virescens,*
Aegira virescens, Castagnea virescens

Class Phaeophyceae

Order Ectocarpales

Family Chordariaceae

North Pacific distribution Alaska Peninsula,
Alaska, to central British Columbia; China; Japan.

Description The thallus of this distinctive species is golden brown, gelatinous, and
has an irregular branching pattern. Thalli generally reach a height of 10 cm (4 in).

Habitat This species is a midsummer annual found on rock, soft substrate, and
epiphytically on other vegetation such as eelgrass in the low intertidal and upper
subtidal zones. This species prefers semi-protected or more sheltered habitats.

Anderson's gooey brown
Haplogloia andersonii (Farlow) Levring

2 cm

Former names *Mesogloia andersonii,*
Myriogloia andersonii

Class Phaeophyceae

Order Ectocarpales

Family Chordariaceae

North Pacific distribution Kodiak archipelago,
Alaska, to Baja California, Mexico.

Description Thallus is dark brown to light tan, soft and mucilaginous, with a hairy
(rarely smooth) appearance due to the many long pigmented hairs, which together
with the much shorter (5-9 cells long) pigmented assimilatory filaments, arise from
the large-celled colorless medulla. Branching is irregular to several orders.

Habitat The species occurs in the mid to low intertidal on semi-protected shores
along the outer coast.

63

False kelp
Petalonia fascia (O.F. Müller) Kuntze

5 cm

Former names *Fucus fascia, Ilea fascia, Petalonia debilis, Phyllitis fascia*

Class Phaeophyceae

Order Ectocarpales

Family Scytosiphonaceae

North Pacific distribution Arctic Ocean, Bering Sea and Aleutian Islands, Alaska, to Baja California, Mexico; China; Korea; Japan; Russia.

Description The thallus is a light to medium brown blade that tapers below to a tiny discoidal holdfast, but lacks the complex cell differentiation of true kelps. The blade is thinner than kelps, and the margins are smooth. The thallus can grow up to 35 cm (14 in) tall.

Habitat This annual is found growing on rock in the mid intertidal to shallow subtidal from protected to semi-exposed habitats.

Similar to young *Laminaria*, young *Saccharina*, *Punctaria*.

Eelgrass brown blade
Punctaria lobata
(D.A. Saunders) Setchell et N.L. Gardner

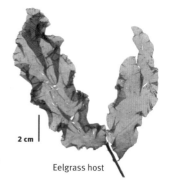

2 cm

Eelgrass host

Former name *Homeostroma lobatum*

Class Phaeophyceae

Order Ectocarpales

Family Chordariaceae

North Pacific distribution Kodiak archipelago to Southeast Alaska.

Description The thallus is a small, pale to dark olive brown blade, 10 cm or more tall, with margins smooth or irregularly to deeply lobed, and is 2-4 cell layers thick, with medullary (central) cells no more than 2-3 times the size of cortical (outer) cells. The outer cells have numerous discoidal chloroplasts and pyrenoids.

Habitat This summer ephemeral occurs as an epiphyte on *Zostera marina* in the mid intertidal to shallow subtidal of protected habitats.

Similar to *Petalonia*, young *Saccharina*.

False kelp *Petalonia fascia*

Eelgrass brown blade *Punctaria lobata*

Brown Seaweeds

Northern bladder chain

Stephanocystis geminata (C. Agardh) Draisma, Ballesteros, F. Rousseau et T. Thibaut

Former names Cystoseira geminata, Cystophyllum geminatum, C. lepidum

Class Phaeophyceae

Order Fucales

Family Sargassaceae

North Pacific distribution Bering Sea and Aleutian Islands, Alaska, to northern Washington; Japan; Russia.

Description The light brown thallus is anchored by a sturdy discoidal holdfast and the stiff stipe branches radially to give rise to several main branches, long secondary branches, and finally short terminal branchlets. The terminal branchlets carry small oval, air-filled bladders (pneumatocysts) that can be single, paired, or in short chains terminating in a small pointed projection. The entire thallus can reach up to 5 m (16 ft) tall and form a canopy.

Habitat This perennial is found on rock in the low intertidal and subtidal zones of semi-exposed habitats.

Similar to *Sargassum**.

Rockweed or popweed

Fucus distichus Linnaeus

Former names *Fucus distichus* subsp. *evanescens*, *F. gardneri*, *F. evanescens*

Class Phaeophyceae

Order Fucales

Family Fucaceae

North Pacific distribution Arctic Ocean, Bering Sea and Aleutian Islands, Alaska, to central California; Japan; Russia.

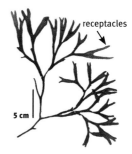

receptacles

5 cm

Description Thallus of this very common and abundant intertidal species is yellow-brown to medium brown, with a discoidal holdfast; flattened, strap-like blades with midribs, which repeatedly branch more or less equally (dichotomous branching); and distinctive air bladders (receptacles) at reproductive maturity. Individuals grow up to 50 cm (20 in) tall.

Habitat This perennial can dominate high to low intertidal rock from estuarine to semi-exposed habitats. Rockweed is very tolerant of fresh water and freezing temperatures.

Northern bladder chain *Stephanocystis geminata*

Rockweed or popweed *Fucus distichus*

Golden V kelp

Aureophycus aleuticus H. Kawai, T. Hanyuda,
M. Lindeberg et S.C. Lindstrom

Class Phaeophyceae

Order Laminariales

Family Aureophycaceae

North Pacific distribution Central Aleutian
Islands and St. George Island, Alaska.

25 cm

Description Thallus of this endemic kelp is light brown with golden yellow edges
at the base of the blade, forming a V pattern. The holdfast is semi-discoidal and the
stipe is flattened, golden in color, and up to 1 m (3.2 ft) in length. The blade is thin,
lanceolate in form, up to 2 m (6.5 ft) long and 0.5 m (20 in) wide.

Habitat This uncommon kelp grows on rock in the shallow subtidal and prefers
semi-exposed or exposed habitats where ocean waves break near the shoreline.

Northern rhizome kelp

Laminaria longipes Bory

Class Phaeophyceae

Order Laminariales

Family Laminariaceae

North Pacific distribution Bering Sea and
Aleutian Islands to Southeast Alaska; northern
Washington; Russia.

5 cm

Description Thallus of this brown kelp has a branched, rhizomatous holdfast,
with numerous stipes arising from the extensive holdfast structure. A long, narrow
blade, less than 5 cm (2 in) wide and up to 50 cm (20 in) long, extends from each
stipe. *Coilodesme fucicola* and *Pyropia gardneri* are common epiphytes along old
blade margins.

Habitat This perennial kelp grows on rock in the low intertidal of semi-exposed to
exposed habitats.

Similar to *Lessoniopsis* also has narrow blades but a different holdfast.

Golden V kelp *Aureophycus aleuticus*

Northern rhizome kelp *Laminaria longipes*

Southern stiff-stiped kelp
Laminaria setchellii P.C. Silva

Former names *Hafgygia andersonii,
Laminaria andersonii*

Class Phaeophyceae

Order Laminariales

Family Laminariaceae

North Pacific distribution Kenai Peninsula,
Alaska, to Baja California, Mexico.

5 cm

Description Thallus is medium to dark brown with a branched holdfast (haptera), a rigid, erect stipe up to 80 cm (2.7 ft) long with microscopic mucilage ducts well inside the stipe tissue, and a thick blade up to 80 cm (31 in) long and 25 cm (10 in) wide. The blade is deeply split almost to the base, forming nearly uniform segments.

Habitat This perennial is found on rock in the extreme low intertidal and upper subtidal and prefers exposed habitats.

Similar to *Saccharina dentigera*, S. groenlandica.*

Arctic suction-cup kelp
Laminaria solidungula J. Agardh

Class Phaeophyceae

Order Laminariales

Family Laminariaceae

North Pacific distribution Arctic Ocean.

5 cm

Description Thallus of this golden to medium brown kelp has a flat blade that can be slightly undulate at the margin, with stipe to ~15 cm long. The holdfast is discoidal. This slow-growing kelp often displays several years of growth, denoted by the constrictions between roundish blade segments. A blade 7 years old can be less than 1 m (39 in) long.

Habitat This perennial kelp occurs on rock in the shallow subtidal.

Similar to *Laminaria yezoensis* also has a discoid holdfast, but it does not occur in the Arctic.

Southern stiff-stiped kelp *Laminaria setchellii*

Arctic suction-cup kelp *Laminaria solidungula*

Suction-cup kelp

Laminaria yezoensis Miyabe

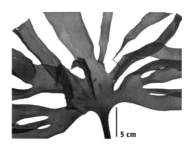

5 cm

Class Phaeophyceae

Order Laminariales

Family Laminariaceae

North Pacific distribution Bering Sea and Aleutian Islands, Alaska, to Johnstone Strait, British Columbia; Japan; Russia.

Description Thallus is medium to dark brown with a large disc or suction cup–like holdfast (see photo inset), a somewhat rigid stipe up to nearly 1 m (37 in) long although it is often shorter, and a thick blade that can be nearly as wide as long. The blade is usually split and has mucilage ducts, which are visible microscopically.

Habitat This perennial kelp is found on rock in the extreme low intertidal to subtidal zones from semi-protected to exposed habitats.

Similar to *Laminaria solidungula*, *Saccharina* spp.

Sugar kelp

Saccharina latissima (Linnaeus) C.E. Lane, C. Mayes, Druehl et G.W. Saunders

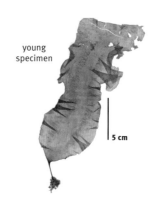

young specimen

5 cm

Former name *Laminaria saccharina*

Class Phaeophyceae

Order Laminariales

Family Laminariaceae

North Pacific distribution Arctic Ocean, Bering Sea and Aleutian Islands, Alaska, to Santa Catalina Island, California; Korea; Japan; Russia.

Description Thallus of this very common kelp is light to medium brown with a finely branched holdfast (haptera), a cylindrical stipe up to 50 cm (20 in) long without mucilage ducts, and a blade up to 3.5 m (10 ft) long. The blade is moderately thin and undulate and frequently has rows of blister-like swellings or puckers (bullations) near the base.

Habitat Although this kelp is considered a perennial, the blade dies back in the fall/winter and re-grows in the spring. It attaches to rock in the low intertidal to subtidal and prefers protected to semi-protected habitats.

Similar to *Saccharina groenlandica*.

Suction-cup kelp *Laminaria yezoensis*

Sugar kelp *Saccharina latissima*

Sea cabbage

Saccharina sessilis (C. Agardh) Kuntze

Former names *Hedophyllum sessile, Laminaria sessilis*

Class Phaeophyceae

Order Laminariales

Family Laminariaceae

North Pacific distribution Aleutian Islands, Alaska, to Monterey County, California; Commander Islands, Russia.

5 cm

Description Thallus of this kelp is unique in that it lacks a stipe. It is medium to dark brown with a branched holdfast (haptera) and a somewhat thick blade up to 1.5 m (5 ft) long. The blade can be bullate (appear puckered) and become torn with age.

Habitat This perennial kelp is found on rock in the mid to low intertidal from semi-protected to semi-exposed habitats. Specimens from more exposed habitats tend to be smooth with many splits.

Similar to *Saccharina groenlandica*.

Split kelp

Saccharina groenlandica (Rosenvinge) C.E. Lane, C. Mayes, Druehl et G.W. Saunders

Former names *Laminaria groenlandica, Saccharina subsimplex*

Class Phaeophyceae

Order Laminariales

Family Laminariaceae

North Pacific distribution Bering Sea and Aleutian Islands, Alaska, to central California; Russia.

young specimen

5 cm

Description Thallus of this common kelp is medium to dark brown with a branched holdfast (haptera), a stipe up to 60 cm (24 in) long with microscopic mucilage ducts, and a blade up to 2 m (6 ft) long. The blade is often bullate (puckered) when young but becomes thicker and smoother with age; it often splits into 2-3 segments. The stipe is cylindrical at the holdfast but is often flattened at the base of the blade.

Habitat This perennial kelp is found on rock in the low intertidal to shallow subtidal zones and occurs in semi-protected to semi-exposed habitats.

Similar to *Laminaria* spp., *Saccharina* spp.

Sea cabbage *Saccharina sessilis*

Split kelp *Saccharina groenlandica*

Spiral sieve kelp

Agarum clathrus (S.G. Gmelin) Greville

5 cm

> **Former names** *Thalassiophyllum clathrus, Fucus clathrus, Laminaria clathrus*
>
> **Class** Phaeophyceae
> **Order** Laminariales
> **Family** Agaraceae
>
> **North Pacific distribution** Pribilof Islands, Aleutian Islands, and Sanak Island, Alaska; Russia.

Description Thallus of this unique kelp is brown with a branched holdfast (haptera) and a woody stipe that is spirally twisted due to meristematic growth from which new blades unfurl. The blade can grow to at least 50 cm (20 in) long and has somewhat regular perforations. Reproductive patches (sori) develop on the older portions of the blade.

Habitat This perennial kelp is found on rock in the very low intertidal and shallow subtidal and prefers semi-exposed habitats. It is also found in tide pools.

Similar to *Agarum fimbriatum*, A. turneri*.*

Spiral sieve kelp

Spiral sieve kelp *Agarum clathrus*

Sori on blades of spiral sieve kelp

Sieve kelp
Agarum clathratum Dumortier

5 cm

Former names *Fucus agarum, F. pertusus, Agarum cribrosum, A. gmelini*

Class Phaeophyceae

Order Laminariales

Family Agaraceae

North Pacific distribution Arctic Ocean and Bering Sea, Alaska, to northern Washington; Korea; Japan; Russia.

Description Thallus of this medium brown kelp has a branched holdfast (haptera), a stipe up to 30 cm (12 in) long, a stiff blade riddled with small, distinctive holes, and a wide midrib. The blade grows to 90 cm (35 in) long and 50 cm (20 in) wide. When present, fertile patches (sori) are found toward the edges of the blade.

Habitat This perennial kelp is found on rock in the very low intertidal to subtidal (to a depth of at least 15 m or 50 ft) and prefers a semi-protected habitat.

Similar to *Agarum fimbriatum*, A. turneri*, A. clathrus.*

Ribbon kelp
Alaria marginata Postels et Ruprecht

sporophyllis

5 cm

Former name *Alaria valida*

Class Phaeophyceae

Order Laminariales

Family Alariaceae

North Pacific distribution Aleutian Islands, Alaska, to Point Conception, California.

Description Thallus of this common intertidal kelp is brown with a branched holdfast (haptera); a stipe, cylindrical near the base but flattened near the blade, that can reach 30 cm (12 in) or more in length; and a thin, lanceolate blade up to 3 m (10 ft) long with solid midrib. Twenty to forty elliptical sporophylls form in spring on the upper portion of the stipe and grow up to 25 cm (10 in) long, thickening with maturity.

Habitat This kelp is an annual found on rock in the mid to low intertidal from semi-protected (if there is sufficient current) to exposed habitats.

Sieve kelp *Agarum clathratum*

Ribbon kelp *Alaria marginata*

Brown Seaweeds

Five-ribbed kelp

Costaria costata (C. Agardh) D.A. Saunders

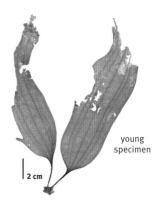

young specimen

2 cm

Former names *Fucus costatus, Agarum costatum, A. quinquecostatum, Laminaria costata, Costaria mertensii, C. turneri*

Class Phaeophyceae
Order Laminariales
Family Agaraceae

North Pacific distribution Unalaska Island, Alaska, to southern California.

Description Thallus of this light to medium brown kelp has a branched holdfast (haptera), a somewhat flattened, finely grooved stipe, and an elliptical blade up to 2 m (6.5 ft) long and 35 cm (14 in) wide with 5 parallel ribs running its length. Three ribs project on one side of the blade and 2 ribs on the other. Between the ribs the blade is profusely wrinkled or puckered.

Habitat This annual kelp is found on rock in the low intertidal to upper subtidal from semi-protected to semi-exposed habitats.

Three-ribbed kelp

Cymathaere triplicata (Postels et Ruprecht) J. Agardh

fertile sori

5 cm

Former name *Laminaria triplicata*

Class Phaeophyceae
Order Laminariales
Family Laminariaceae

North Pacific distribution Bering Sea and Aleutian Islands, Alaska, to northern Washington; Russia.

Description Thallus of this light to sometimes reddish brown kelp has a discoidal holdfast, a stipe up to 25 cm (10 in) long, a linear blade up to 4 m (13 ft) long and 18 cm (7 in) wide, and three riblike folds. No other kelp has this configuration. This species has a distinctive cucumber-like aroma that can often be smelled before the kelp is seen, but the species is not palatable.

Habitat This annual kelp grows on rock (often cobble) in the low intertidal to upper subtidal from semi-protected to semi-exposed habitats.

Five-ribbed kelp *Costaria costata*

Three-ribbed kelp *Cymathaere triplicata*

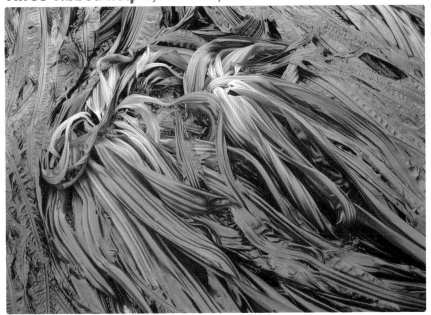

Flat pompom kelp

Lessoniopsis littoralis (Farlow et Setchell ex Tilden) Reinke

Former name *Lessonia littoralis*

Class Phaeophyceae
Order Laminariales
Family Alariaceae

North Pacific distribution Kodiak archipelago, Alaska, to Monterey County, California.

|5 cm

Description Thallus of this medium to dark brown kelp has a branched holdfast (haptera) and a trunk-like stipe that is profusely dichotomously branched, with each branch terminating in a strap-like blade with midrib. This kelp can reach 2 m (6.5 ft) long. Reproductive sporophylls are located near the base of older blades.

Habitat This perennial kelp is found on rock in the very low intertidal to shallow subtidal in exposed habitats.

Similar to *Laminaria longipes* also has clustered strap-like blades but a rhizomatous holdfast.

Broad-ribbed kelp

Pleurophycus gardneri Setchell et D.A. Saunders ex Tilden

Class Phaeophyceae
Order Laminariales
Family Alariaceae

North Pacific distribution Kodiak archipelago, Alaska, to Monterey County, California.

|5 cm

Description Thallus of this dark brown kelp has a branched holdfast (haptera); a stipe, cylindrical at the base, flattening above, up to 50 cm (20 in) long; and an elliptical blade to 150 cm (60 in) long and 28 cm (11 in) wide with a distinctive thick, broad midrib 5 cm (1.75 in) wide. The blade is puckered along the sides of the midrib. The stipe and holdfast are perennial while the blade is annual and dies back in the fall.

Habitat This species occurs on rock in the extreme low intertidal and upper subtidal of semi-exposed habitats or high current areas.

Flat pompom kelp *Lessoniopsis littoralis*

Broad-ribbed kelp *Pleurophycus gardneri*

Dragon kelp
Eualaria fistulosa
(Postels et Ruprecht) M.J. Wynne

Former names *Alaria fistulosa*, *Druehlia fistulosa*

Class Phaeophyceae

Order Laminariales

Family Alariaceae

North Pacific distribution Aleutian Islands to southern Southeast Alaska; Japan; Russia.

sporophylls

air filled midrib

5 cm

haptera

Description Thallus of this canopy-forming kelp is brown with a large branching holdfast (haptera), a stipe 25 cm (10 in) long, and a blade with midrib up to 25 m (82 ft) long and 1 m (3.2 ft) wide. The midrib is 2-3 cm (0.8-1.2 in) wide with gas-filled chambers (fistulae) that hold the blade in the water column. Reproductive sporophylls develop on the upper portion of the stipe.

Habitat This fast growing annual occurs on rock from the low intertidal to subtidal and forms offshore kelp beds in cold, semi-protected to exposed habitats.

Dragon kelp

Dragon kelp *Eualaria fistulosa*

Giant kelp

Macrocystis pyrifera (Linnaeus) C. Agardh

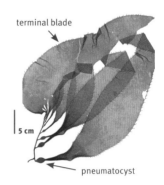

terminal blade

5 cm

pneumatocyst

Former name *Fucus pyriferus*

Class Phaeophyceae
Order Laminariales
Family Laminariaceae

North Pacific distribution Kodiak archipelago, Alaska, to Baja California, Mexico.

Description Thallus of this golden brown canopy kelp may reach a length of 30 m (99 ft). A conical, richly branched holdfast (haptera) hosts several stipes, which branch dichotomously into vine-like fronds with blades to ~50 cm (20 in) long at regular intervals. The blades, which develop via splitting of a small terminal blade, are distinctly wrinkled with marginal teeth and a small gas-filled float (pneumatocyst) at their base.

Habitat This perennial kelp forms beds in the extreme low intertidal to subtidal of semi-exposed habitats.

Similar to This species is considered by some to be the same species as *Macrocystis integrifolia**.

Giant kelp

Giant kelp *Macrocystis pyrifera*

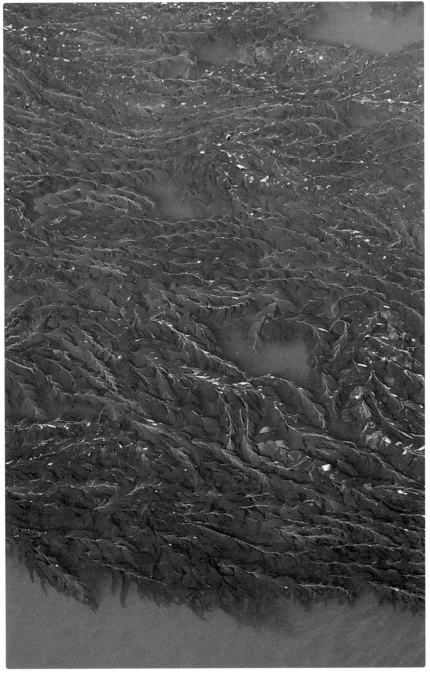

Bull kelp
Nereocystis luetkeana
(K. Mertens) Postels et Ruprecht

> **Former name** *Fucus luetkeanus*
>
> **Class** Phaeophyceae
> **Order** Laminariales
> **Family** Laminariaceae
>
> **North Pacific distribution** Eastern Aleutian Islands (Umnak Island), Alaska, to San Luis Obispo County, California.

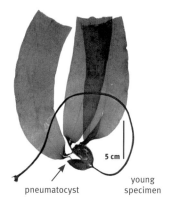

5 cm

pneumatocyst   young specimen

Description Thallus of this common canopy-forming kelp has a richly branched holdfast (haptera) and a cylindrical stipe 10-36 m (33-118 ft) long, terminating in a single, gas-filled pneumatocyst from which the many blades, up to 10 m (33 ft) long, develop. Blade growth can reach 15 cm (6 in) per day. Reproductive patches (sori) develop on the blades and drop to the seafloor at maturity.

Habitat This annual kelp grows on rock from the low intertidal to subtidal; it prefers semi-exposed habitats or high current areas. Offshore beds can persist for one to many years, usually in deeper water than *Eualaria* or *Macrocystis*, where they co-occur.

Bull kelp with sori patches

sori

Bull kelp *Nereocystis luetkeana*

Fringed sieve kelp
Agarum fimbriatum Harvey

North Pacific distribution Southeast Alaska to Baja California, Mexico.

Description Thallus is an elliptical, rather thin brown blade to 80 cm (31 in) long, with a puckered appearance; scattered, irregular holes; and a faint midrib basally. The holdfast is of narrow, branched haptera; the stipe is flattened, 2-6 cm (1-4 in) long, and has numerous projections (fimbriations) along the margin. This perennial is usually found in the subtidal zone to 20 m (66 ft) depth in semi-protected to semi-exposed habitats.

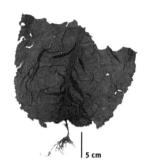

5 cm

Smooth sieve kelp
Agarum turneri Postels et Ruprecht

North Pacific distribution Aleutian Islands to Cook Inlet, Alaska; Japan; Russia.

Description Thallus is a smooth, ovate brown blade to 90 cm (35 in) long and 30 cm (14 in) wide with a flattened midrib, large circular holes, and a branched holdfast. The species occurs subtidally to at least 20 m depth in semi-exposed habitats. It is currently considered by many phycologists not to be a separate species from *Agarum clathratum*, but it is morphologically distinct.

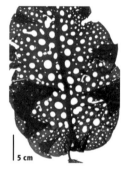

5 cm

Kelp fringe
Coilodesme fucicola (Yendo) Nagai

North Pacific distribution Aleutian Islands to western Gulf of Alaska; Russia.

Description Thallus is a flattened, obovate to elongate, light brown sac, with a narrow stipe, to 13 cm (5 in) tall and 0.8 cm (0.3 in) wide, attached by an inconspicuous discoidal holdfast. This species grows in abundance along the margin of kelps, particularly *Laminaria longipes*, in the low intertidal of semi-exposed habitats.

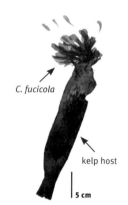

C. fucicola

kelp host

5 cm

Bulb seaweed
Colpomenia peregrina Sauvageau

North Pacific distribution Aleutian Islands, Alaska, to southern California; Korea; Japan; Russia.

Description Thallus is golden brown, globular, reaching 7 cm (3 in) in diameter. The thin, smooth hollow thallus tears easily. The thallus also has colorless hairs in clusters on its surface. This annual grows either directly on rock or on other algae in the low intertidal in semi-exposed to semi-protected habitats.

Flattened acid kelp
Desmarestia ligulata (Stackhouse) J.V. Lamouroux

North Pacific distribution Unalaska Island, Alaska, to Baja California, Mexico; Korea; Japan; Russia.

Description Thallus is golden to olive brown, ligulate, reaching 80 cm (31 in) tall, with opposite, flattened branches to several orders and a main axis and branches with faint midrib and lateral veins. This annual occurs in the low intertidal and subtidal of semi-protected to semi-exposed habitats. This species has a high acid content and causes specimens to quickly break down.

Diatom mats

North Pacific distribution Widely distributed.

Description Commonly mistaken for a filamentous brown seaweed, diatom mats do not have true filaments or branching. They can easily be broken up when rolled between the fingers. They prefer areas that are always damp, such as creeks or stream channels, especially in estuarine habitats.

Feather boa kelp
Egregia menziesii (Turner) Areschoug

> **North Pacific distribution** Southern Southeast Alaska to Baja California, Mexico.

Description Thallus is strap-shaped, dark brown to olive green, covered with dense papillae and bearing small blades and air bladders along the margins of the straps. The species is usually less than 4.5 m (15 ft) long. Holdfast is conical, compact, and richly branched (haptera). The species is a perennial occurring in the low intertidal to subtidal zones of semi-exposed habitats.

Rockweed tuft
Elachista fucicola (Velley) Areschoug

> **North Pacific distribution** Arctic Ocean and Alaska Peninsula, Alaska, to northern California; Russia.

Description Thallus is a tuft of mostly unbranched, pigmented, uniseriate filaments growing on *Fucus*, up to 0.7 cm (0.28 in) tall. Large, elongate unilocular sporangia commonly occur on colorless branched basal filaments, but these can be seen only with a microscope. This species can co-occur with *Pylaiella littoralis*, which is usually much longer and is always branched.

Small perennial kelp
Macrocystis integrifolia Bory

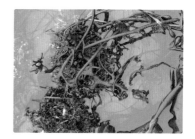

> **North Pacific distribution** Southeast Alaska to Monterey Peninsula, California.

Description Thallus is similar to *Macrocystis pyrifera* but distinguished by a flattened, creeping, rhizome-like holdfast, with branched haptera arising from numerous points along the margin of the rhizome. The species is considered by some to be the same as *Macrocystis pyrifera*. It occurs in the lowest intertidal and shallow subtidal on semi-protected to semi-exposed shores with full salinity.

Woody-stemmed kelp
Pterygophora californica Ruprecht

5 cm

> **North Pacific distribution** Cook Inlet, Alaska, to Baja California, Mexico.

Description Thallus has a stiff, woody stipe to 1.5 m (60 in) long and bladelike sporophylls attached along the flattened distal margins of the stipe, which usually terminates in a small, smooth blade with a faint midrib. This tough kelp can reach 2.3 m (7.5 ft) tall. It is a long-lived perennial, usually found only on rock, including cobble, in the subtidal zone (7-20 m, 23-66 ft) of more exposed coasts.

Northern stiff-stiped kelp
Saccharina dentigera (Kjellman) C.E. Lane, C. Mayes, Druehl et G.W. Saunders

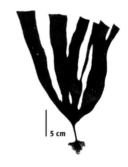

5 cm

> **North Pacific distribution** Bering Sea and Aleutian Islands, Alaska, to western Gulf of Alaska; Russia.

Description Thallus is dark brown, thick, reaching 1.5 m (5 ft) tall. The holdfast is branched, the stipe somewhat rigid, and the blade often split down to 10 cm (4 in) above its base. Mucilage ducts occur near the surface of stipe. This perennial is found on rock in the very low intertidal to shallow subtidal.

Wireweed
Sargassum muticum (Yendo) Fensholt

5 cm

> **North Pacific distribution** Southern Southeast Alaska to Baja California, Mexico; Japan.

Description Thallus is golden brown, wiry, bushy, reaching 3 m (9 ft) tall, with a main axis and alternate branching and attached by a small discoidal holdfast. The small blades have toothed margins, and small rounded floats usually occur singly and lack a pointed tip. An invasive perennial accidentally introduced from Japan, it occurs mainly in the low intertidal and shallow subtidal of protected to semi-exposed habitats.

Red Seaweeds

Phylum Rhodophyta

The Rhodophyta is a unique group of organisms, which, like the Chlorophyta, are thought to be very ancient. Most red algae belong to the class Florideophyceae, which is characterized by proteinaceous "pit" plugs occluding the connection between cells (due to incomplete cell cleavage at mitosis). Most red algae are multicellular and marine, but unicellular and freshwater taxa also occur. No red algal cell, including reproductive cells, is flagellated. Like the Chlorophyta, the chloroplast is encircled by a double membrane, but thylakoids occur singly and are not stacked. The primary pigment is chlorophyll *a*, and cells are distinctively colored by the accessory pigments, phycocyanin and phycoerythrin, which occur in hemispheric granules on the thylakoids. The photosynthetic product is a highly branched form of starch and is stored outside the chloroplast.

Long laver (*Pyropia* sp.).

Common forms of red seaweeds

Fleshy crusts

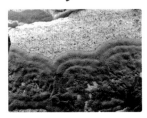

Rusty rock
  Hildenbrandia rubra 98
Tar spot alga
  Mastocarpus spp.
  Petrocelis phase 98

Turf forming

Sea moss
  Endocladia muricata 100
Jelly moss
  Gloiopeltis furcata 100
Red sea moss
  Rhodochorton purpureum 102

Corallines

Enigmatic coral seaweed
  Bossiella frondescens 104
Graceful coral seaweed
  Corallina vancouveriensis 104
Chalky coral seaweed
  Corallina officinalis 106
Coralline disc
  *Neopolyporolithon
  reclinatum* 106
Thick rock crust
  *Clathromorphum
  nereostratum 108*
Rock crusts 108

Tubes or Sacs

Sea sac
  Halosaccion glandiforme 110
Flattened sea sac
  Halosaccion firmum 110
Ephemeral sea sac[1]
  Halosaccion sp. 112
Purple pencils
  Dumontia alaskana[1] 112

[1]species found only in Alaska

Common forms of red seaweeds

Finely branched

Pretty polly
  Polysiphonia pacifica 114
Black tassel
  Pterosiphonia bipinnata 114
Hooked skein
  Antithamnionella pacifica 116
Scagel's skein
  Scagelia occidentalis 116
Alternate skein
  *Pleonosporium
  vancouverianum* 117
Staghorn felt
  Ceramium pacificum 117

Coarsely branched

Bushy Ahnfelt's seaweed
  Ahnfeltia fastigiata 118
Beauty bush
  Callithamnion pikeanum 118
Bleached brunette
  Cryptosiphonia woodii 120
Coarse sea lace
  Microcladia borealis 120
Graceful black pine
  Neorhodomela aculeata 122
Black pine
  Neorhodomela larix 122
Oregon pine
  Neorhodomela oregona 124
Sea brush
  Odonthalia floccosa 124
Sea fern
  Neoptilota asplenioides 126
Northern sea fern
  Ptilota serrata 126

Thin blades

Seagrass laver
  Smithora naiadum 128
Dark laver
  Fuscifolium papenfussii 128
Black seaweed
  Pyropia abbottiae 129
Summer laver[1]
  Boreophyllum aestivale 130
Red cellophane
  Wildemania amplissima 130

---

[1]species found only in Alaska

Thin blades (continued)

Thick blades

Blades with ribs or veins

Other forms

Rusty rock
Hildenbrandia rubra (Sommerfelt) Meneghini

Former names *Verrucaria rubra,*
Hildenbrandia prototypus, H. rosea

Class Florideophyceae
Order Hildenbrandiales
Family Hildenbrandiaceae

North Pacific distribution Arctic Ocean, Bering Sea
and Aleutian Islands, Alaska, to Panama; China; Russia.

Description Thallus is a rose-to-brownish-red, uncalcified crust that adheres tightly
to rock. It is very thin (0.3 mm or 0.01 in thick), can appear partly transparent,
and grows very slowly. Tetrasporangia, which are irregularly divided and occur in
conceptacles, are the only known form of reproduction.

Habitat Found throughout the year on emergent rock and in tide pools from the high
intertidal to shallow subtidal of protected to exposed habitats.

Similar to *Hildenbrandia occidentalis*[†] has regularly zonately divided tetrasporangia;
also similar to basal crusts of *Gloiopeltis* and *Palmaria*.

Tar spot alga
Mastocarpus spp. (Petrocelis phase)

Former names *Petrocelis franciscana,*
P. middendorffii

Class Florideophyceae
Order Gigartinales
Family Phyllophoraceae

North Pacific distribution Bering Sea and Aleutian
Islands, Alaska, to Baja California, Mexico; Japan; Russia.

Description Thallus is a thick (to 2 mm or 0.08 in), brownish to blackish crust that
is actually the alternate reproductive phase (tetrasporophyte) of Turkish washcloth
(*Mastocarpus*). The crust is firm but not hard: one can sink one's fingernail into it. Its
surface is smooth but sometimes shows faint concentric scalloping.

Habitat This very resilient, perennial phase can be extremely long-lived, to 90+
years; common on high to low intertidal rock in protected to semi-exposed habitats.

Similar to *Ralfsia* spp., tar spots from stranded oil.

Rusty rock *Hildenbrandia rubra*

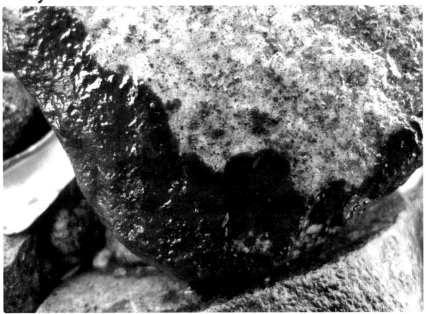

Tar spot alga *Mastocarpus* spp. (Petrocelis phase)

Sea moss

Endocladia muricata (Endlicher) J. Agardh

> **Former names** *Acanthocladia muricata, Gelidium muricatum, Gigartina muricata*

> **Class** Florideophyceae
> **Order** Gigartinales
> **Family** Endocladiaceae

> **North Pacific distribution** Aleutian Islands, Alaska, to Baja California, Mexico.

2 cm

Description Thallus is rusty red to black (when dry); its wiry, cylindrical branches have spines and form small bushy tufts 3-8 cm tall (1-3 in). This perennial has isomorphic or similar-looking reproductive phases.

Habitat This species forms a band on rocks in the high to mid intertidal zone of semi-exposed to exposed habitats.

Similar to *Gloiopeltis furcata*; *Caulacanthus ustulatus*[†] (not confirmed to occur in Alaska; *Endocladia muricata* can develop creeping portions similar to *Caulacanthus ustulatus* in late summer).

Jelly moss

Gloiopeltis furcata (Postels et Ruprecht) J. Agardh

> **Former name** *Dumontia furcata*

> **Class** Florideophyceae
> **Order** Gigartinales
> **Family** Endocladiaceae

> **North Pacific distribution** Bering Sea and Aleutian Islands, Alaska, to Baja California, Mexico; China; Taiwan; Korea; Japan; Russia.

2 cm

Description Thallus is rusty red to golden yellow, up to 5 cm (2 in) tall. The smooth, narrow cylindrical branches fork infrequently and are more or less dichotomous; they lack spines and have a rubbery to slippery texture. The annual thallus grows from a perennial basal crust each spring.

Habitat A less hearty alga than sea moss, with which it can co-occur, jelly moss is common on rock in the high to mid intertidal in protected to semi-exposed habitats.

Similar to *Endocladia*; basal crust similar to *Hildenbrandia* and to basal crust of *Palmaria*.

Sea moss *Endocladia muricata*

Jelly moss *Gloiopeltis furcata*

Red Seaweeds

Red sea moss

Rhodochorton purpureum (Lightfoot) Rosenvinge

Former names *Audouinella purpurea, Byssus purpurea, Rhodochorton rothii, R. tenue*

Class Florideophyceae

Order Acrochaetiales

Family Acrochaetiaceae

North Pacific distribution Arctic Ocean, Bering Sea and Aleutian Islands, Alaska, to Baja California, Mexico; Japan; Russia.

2 cm

Description Thallus forms purplish-red turfs of erect, very fine, sparingly branched filaments 5-10 mm (0.2-0.4 in) tall. Filaments are densely intertwined basally.

Habitat Turfs occur in the high intertidal on the walls of sea caves or in shady rock crevices, also on mid to low intertidal rock in sheltered to semi-exposed habitats.

Similar to *Sphacelaria rigidula** also forms carpets of short filaments in the intertidal, but it is a brown alga.

Red sea moss *Rhodochorton purpureum*

Enigmatic coral seaweed

Bossiella frondescens (Postels et Ruprecht) E.Y. Dawson

2 cm

Former names *Corallina frondescens,
Arthrocardia frondescens, Cheilosporum
frondescens*

Class Florideophyceae
Order Corallinales
Family Corallinaceae

North Pacific distribution Bering Sea and
Aleutian Islands, Alaska, to Mexico; Russia.

Description Thallus is calcareous, articulated, appearing light pink to light purple
and reaching 3.5 cm (1.4 in) tall from a basal crust. Branching is feather-like
(pinnate) to somewhat irregular. Axial segments are ≤1 mm (0.04 in) long, flattened,
and winged, with terminal segments often broadly expanded, and occasional basal
and terminal cylindrical sections.

Habitat One of Alaska's most common corallines, this species occurs on emergent
rock and in tide pools in the mid to low intertidal of protected to exposed habitats.

Similar to *Bossiella* spp.*, *Corallina* spp.

Graceful coral seaweed

Corallina vancouveriensis Yendo

2 cm

Former name *Corallina densa*

Class Florideophyceae
Order Corallinales
Family Corallinaceae

North Pacific distribution Bering Sea and
Aleutian Islands, Alaska, to Baja California,
Mexico; Japan.

Description Thallus is calcareous, articulated, light pink to light purple, forming
dense tufts to 6 or more cm (2.4 in) tall from a basal crust. Branching is pinnate to
verticillate, and dense. Axial segments are 1 mm long and more or less cylindrical.
Reproductive conceptacles are located at tips of branches but are rare.

Habitat This species forms dense mats on emergent bedrock or in tide pools in the
mid to low intertidal zones of exposed habitats.

Similar to *Bossiella frondescens*, *Corallina* sp.

Enigmatic coral seaweed *Bossiella frondescens*

Graceful coral seaweed *Corallina vancouveriensis*

Chalky coral seaweed
Corallina officinalis Linnaeus

Former names *Pachyarthron cretaceum, Amphiroa cretacea, Amphiroa epiphlegmoides, Arthrocardia cretacea, Bossiella cretacea, Corallina cretacea*

Class Florideophyceae

Order Corallinales

Family Corallinaceae

North Pacific distribution Bering Sea and Aleutian Islands, Alaska, to northern Washington; Japan; Russia.

Description Thallus is calcareous, articulated, purplish/grayish-pink, reaching 7 cm (3 in) tall from a calcareous crust. Branching is irregular with occasional dichotomies; segments are cylindrical, 2-4 mm long and 1-1.5 mm diameter. Reproductive conceptacles occur laterally on axial segments; only male conceptacles sometimes occur at branch tips.

Habitat Commonly found in mid intertidal pools, the low intertidal and subtidal zones from semi-protected to semi-exposed habitats.

Similar to *Calliarthron tuberculosum*[†], *Corallina* sp.

Coralline disc
Neopolyporolithon reclinatum (Foslie) W.H. Adey et H.W. Johansen

Former names *Clathromorphum reclinatum, Lithothamnion conchatum* f. *reclinatum, L. reclinatum, Polyporolithon reclinatum*

Class Florideophyceae

Order Corallinales

Family Hapalidiaceae

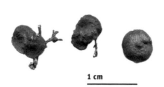

North Pacific distribution Aleutian Islands, Alaska, to southern California; Japan; Russia.

Description A calcareous epiphyte usually found on articulated coralline algae and *Ahnfeltia*, this brownish-pink, discoidal crust is 1.5 cm (0.6 in) diameter and up to 1 mm (0.04 in) thick. It attaches to the host with small pads of tissue rather than a stalk.

Habitat This species is commonly found attached to host algae in tide pools and the low intertidal to shallow subtidal zones of semi-exposed to exposed habitats.

Similar to *Mesophyllum conchatum*[†] (not confirmed north of British Columbia).

Chalky coral seaweed *Corallina officinalis*

Coralline disc *Neopolyporolithon reclinatum*

Thick rock crust
Clathromorphum nereostratum Lebednik

> **Class** Florideophyceae
>
> **Order** Corallinales
>
> **Family** Hapalidiaceae
>
> **North Pacific distribution** Aleutian Islands, Alaska; Kurile Islands, Russia.

Description Thallus is a calcareous crust, light pink to purplish-red, with a smooth chalky surface. Margins are whitish, thick, free, and overgrowing. The largest species in the genus, it can form crusts up to 50 cm (20 in) thick and 1 m or more (39 in) in diameter. Growth rings can be seen in cross section. This represents several hundred years of growth and provides extensive habitat for boring organisms.

Habitat This species is found growing on rock in the low intertidal to a depth of at least 30 m (100 ft) in semi-exposed to exposed habitats.

Similar to *Clathromorphum compactum*[†].

Rock crusts
Clathromorphum sp., *Leptophytum* sp.[†], *Lithophyllum* sp.[†], *Lithothamnion* sp.[†], *Mesophyllum* sp.[†], *Pseudolithophyllum* sp.[†]

> **Class** Florideophyceae
>
> **Order** Corallinales
>
> **Family** Hapalidiaceae
>
> **North Pacific distribution** Throughout the area.

Description This group encompasses calcareous species that form extensive, thin, pink or purplish crusts (white when dead). Crusts usually are 1-5 mm thick, and their surface can appear smooth, pitted, or have rounded protuberances.

Habitat These perennial crusts are found on rock or shell in the high intertidal (uncommon) to the low intertidal and subtidal (very common) of semi-protected to exposed habitats.

Thick rock crust *Clathromorphum nereostratum*

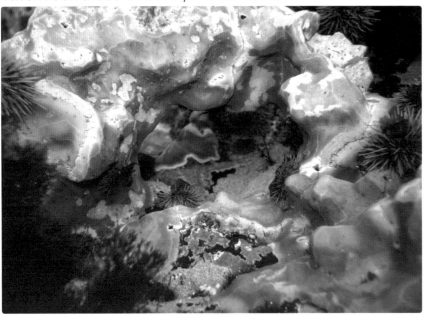

Rock crusts

Sea sac
Halosaccion glandiforme (S.G. Gmelin) Ruprecht

Former names *Ulva glandiformis,
Halosaccion decapitatum, H. fucicola*

Class Florideophyceae
Order Palmariales
Family Palmariaceae

2 cm

North Pacific distribution Chukchi Sea,
Bering Sea and Aleutian Islands, Alaska, to
Point Conception, California; Russia.

Description Thallus is saccate, reddish purple to yellowish brown, tapering to a
short stipe and a small discoidal holdfast and reaching 15 cm (6 in) tall but usually
shorter. Tiny pores allow seawater inside the sac to spray outward when the thallus
is squeezed.

Habitat This annual usually grows in clumps on rock or epiphytically on other algae
in the mid to low intertidal of semi-protected to exposed habitats (high intertidal
patch-forming and tide-pool specimens are probably not this species).

Similar to *Halosaccion* spp.

Flattened sea sac
Halosaccion firmum (Postels et Ruprecht) Kützing

Former name *Dumontia firma*

Class Florideophyceae
Order Palmariales
Family Palmariaceae

2 cm

North Pacific distribution Alaska Peninsula to
Prince William Sound, Alaska; Russia.

Description Thallus is reddish purple, with a dozen or more flattened, hollow blades
arising from the margin of a central linear sac, all tapering to a short stipe. The
thallus, attached by a small discoidal holdfast, reaches 8 cm (3 in) tall but is usually
shorter.

Habitat This annual or biennial species usually grows on rock (including cobble) in
the low intertidal to upper subtidal of protected to semi-exposed habitats.

Similar to *Palmaria* and *Opuntiella* are not hollow; *Halosaccion* spp. are not
compressed.

Sea sac *Halosaccion glandiforme*

Flattened sea sac *Halosaccion firmum*

Ephemeral sea sac

***Halosaccion* sp.** (undescribed)

> **Class** Florideophyceae
>
> **Order** Palmariales
>
> **Family** Palmariaceae
>
> **North Pacific distribution** Lower Cook Inlet, Alaska.

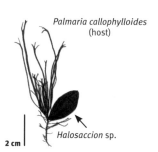

Palmaria callophylloides (host)

Halosaccion sp.

2 cm

Description Thallus is saccate, with or without a short stipe, nearly spherical to elliptical, and reaches 3.5 cm (1.4 in) tall and 2 cm (0.8 in) wide although usually smaller, and growing singly or in clusters. Color is dark rose pink. Thallus is very thin and easily tears.

Habitat This ephemeral is known only from spring collections growing on *Palmaria callophylloides* and *P. hecatensis* in the lower mid intertidal of semi-exposed habitats.

Similar to Other *Halosaccion* species are more robust and are not epiphytic on other Palmariaceae.

Purple pencils

Dumontia alaskana V. Tai, S.C. Lindstrom et G.W. Saunders

> **Misidentified as** *Dumontia contorta*, *D. incrassata*, *D. filiformis*
>
> **Class** Florideophyceae
>
> **Order** Gigartinales
>
> **Family** Dumontiaceae
>
> **North Pacific distribution** Aleutian Islands to Southeast Alaska.

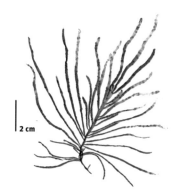

2 cm

Description The dark red to pale pink, partially hollow, contorted, and tubular thallus reaches 27 cm (11 in) tall, with a single order of slightly narrower and shorter, irregularly placed branches.

Habitat A spring annual often gone by June, it is found on rock in mid intertidal pools of semi-exposed to protected habitats.

Similar to Hollow forms of *Palmaria callophylloides* have a more papery texture and are usually more proliferously branched.

Ephemeral sea sac *Halosaccion* sp.

Purple pencils *Dumontia alaskana*

Pretty polly
Polysiphonia pacifica Hollenberg

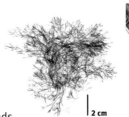
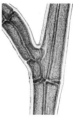

Class Florideophyceae

Order Ceramiales

Family Rhodomelaceae

North Pacific distribution Aleutian Islands, Alaska, to Baja California, Mexico.

2 cm

polysiphonous

Description Thallus is delicate, radially branched, light to dark red, and growing to 30 cm (12 in) tall. This species requires a microscope for accurate identification of polysiphonous branches (4 pericentral cells surrounding the axial cell) and lack of trichoblasts. Tip of each branch is capped with a rounded cell.

Habitat This perennial is found on rock or on other organisms in the low intertidal to subtidal of protected to semi-exposed habitats.

Similar to *Polysiphonia* spp.[†], *Pterosiphonia hamata**, *Antithamnionella pacifica*.

Black tassel
Pterosiphonia bipinnata
(Postels et Ruprecht) Falkenberg

Former names *Polysiphonia bipinnata*, *Pterosiphonia robusta*

Class Florideophyceae

Order Ceramiales

Family Rhodomelaceae

North Pacific distribution Bering Sea and Aleutian Islands, Alaska, to San Pedro, California; Japan; Russia.

2 cm

Description Thallus is fine, profusely branched, dark red to reddish-brown, reaching at least 12 cm (5 in) tall. Branching near tips is all in one plane, spreading out easily on your finger. This species requires a microscope for accurate identification of its polysiphonous habit of 10-12 pericentral cells surrounding the axial cell.

Habitat This common perennial grows on rock in the mid to low intertidal of protected to semi-exposed habitats in spring, but gets grazed back by herbivores.

Similar to *Polysiphonia* spp.[†], *Antithamnionella pacifica*.

Pretty polly *Polysiphonia pacifica*

Black tassel *Pterosiphonia bipinnata*

Hooked skein

Antithamnionella pacifica (Harvey) E.M. Wollaston

Former names *Callithamnion floccosum* var. *pacificum, Antithamnion pacificum, A. uncinatum, A. alternans, A. asymmetricum, Antithamnionella pacifica* var. *uncinata*

Class Florideophyceae

Order Ceramiales

Family Ceramiaceae

North Pacific distribution Aleutian Islands, Alaska, to Baja California, Mexico; Russia.

2 cm

Description Thallus is a delicate, uniseriate filament, reaching 15 cm (6 in) tall. Microscopic branches are opposite, usually short and unbranched, with squarish basal cells. The branch tip is somewhat sinusoidal.

Habitat This ephemeral seaweed grows on rock and epiphytically in the low intertidal and subtidal of semi-protected to exposed habitats.

Similar to *Polysiphonia pacifica, Pterosiphonia* spp.*, *Scagelia occidentalis*

Scagel's skein

Scagelia occidentalis (Kylin) E.M. Wollaston

Former names *Antithamnion occidentale, A. simulans*

Class Florideophyceae

Order Ceramiales

Family Ceramiaceae

North Pacific distribution Arctic Ocean, Bering Sea and Aleutian Islands, Alaska, to southern California.

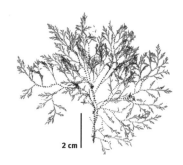

2 cm

Description Thallus is a very fine, red, uniseriate filament with three or four branches of different lengths arising from each axial cell. Gland cells are very common.

Habitat This annual grows on rock, other algae, or even animals in the low intertidal and subtidal of protected to exposed habitats.

Similar to *Antithamnionella, Hollenbergia[†], Pterothamnion[†], Tokidaea[†]*.

Alternate skein

Pleonosporium vancouverianum
(J. Agardh) Setchell et N.L. Gardner

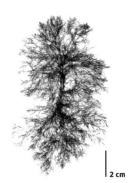

2 cm

> **Former name** *Callithamnion vancouverianum*
>
> **Class** Florideophyceae
> **Order** Ceramiales
> **Family** Wrangeliaceae
>
> **North Pacific distribution** Prince William Sound, Alaska, to Baja California, Mexico.

Description Thallus is a diminutive, uniseriate filament, alternately branched to several orders and less than 2 cm (1 in) tall. This species produces polysporangia rather than tetrasporangia.

Habitat It is an annual and grows on rock, other algae, and on animals in the low intertidal to subtidal of semi-protected to semi-exposed habitats.

Similar to *Callithamnion* spp.[†]

Staghorn felt

Ceramium pacificum (Collins) Kylin

2 cm

> **Former name** *Ceramium rubrum* var. *pacificum*
>
> **Class** Florideophyceae
> **Order** Ceramiales
> **Family** Ceramiaceae
>
> **North Pacific distribution** Alaska Peninsula, Alaska, to Baja California, Mexico.

Description Thallus is red, to 15 cm (6 in) tall, dichotomously or irregularly branched, with paired branch tips forcipate or spreading. Short proliferous branches often present along main axis. Small cells cover the large central axial cell, causing alternate light and dark bands when thallus is held up to light.

Habitat This species grows on rock and epiphytically in the mid to low intertidal of protected to semi-exposed habitats.

Similar to *Microcladia borealis*.

117

Bushy Ahnfelt's seaweed
Ahnfeltia fastigiata (Endlicher) Makienko

Former names *Gigartina fastigiata*

Class Florideophyceae

Order Ahnfeltiales

Family Ahnfeltiaceae

North Pacific distribution Bering Sea and Aleutian Islands, Alaska, to northern Baja California, Mexico; Korea; Japan; Russia.

2 cm

Description Thallus is wiry, dark purple to black, growing in tufts to 15 cm (6 in) tall. Branches are repeatedly dichotomously branched, to 0.5 mm (0.02 in) diameter.

Habitat This tough perennial is slow growing and found on rock, often associated with sand, in the mid to low intertidal of semi-exposed to semi-protected habitats.

Similar to *Ahnfeltia plicata*† looks identical but occurs from the Bering Sea north.

Beauty bush
Callithamnion pikeanum Harvey

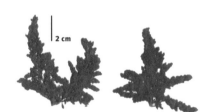

Former names *Callithamnion pikeanum* var. *pacificum*, *C. arborescens*

2 cm

Class Florideophyceae

Order Ceramiales

Family Callithamniaceae

North Pacific distribution Aleutian Islands, Alaska, to southern California; Commander Islands, Russia.

Description Thallus is branched, reddish brown, growing to 10 cm (4 in) tall. Branching is alternate (although appearing radial), dense, giving the thallus a somewhat "woolly" appearance; the uniseriate branches develop a covering of pigmented cells (cortication) except for the ends of the branches, which remain uncovered and terminate in pointed tips.

Habitat This perennial is found on bedrock in the high to mid (rarely low) intertidal of semi-exposed to exposed habitats.

Bushy Ahnfelt's seaweed *Ahnfeltia fastigiata*

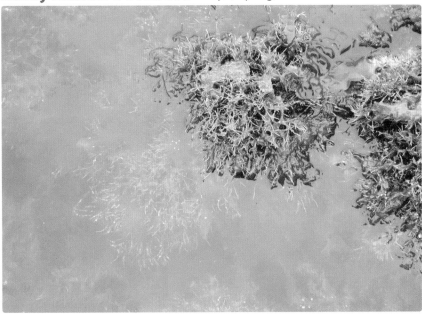

Beauty bush *Callithamnion pikeanum*

Bleached brunette
Cryptosiphonia woodii (J. Agardh) J. Agardh

Former names *Pikea woodii*, *Cryptosiphonia grayana*

Class Florideophyceae

Order Gigartinales

Family Dumontiaceae

North Pacific distribution Unalaska Island, Alaska, to San Pedro, California.

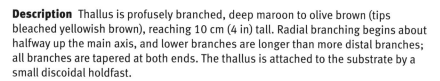

2 cm

Description Thallus is profusely branched, deep maroon to olive brown (tips bleached yellowish brown), reaching 10 cm (4 in) tall. Radial branching begins about halfway up the main axis, and lower branches are longer than more distal branches; all branches are tapered at both ends. The thallus is attached to the substrate by a small discoidal holdfast.

Habitat This annual often grows in dense tufts and is found on rock in the mid to low intertidal of protected to semi-exposed habitats.

Similar to *Neorhodomela oregona*.

Coarse sea lace
Microcladia borealis Ruprecht

Class Florideophyceae

Order Ceramiales

Family Ceramiaceae

North Pacific distribution Aleutian Islands, Alaska, to San Luis Obispo County, California; Commander Islands, Russia.

2 cm

Description Thallus is profusely branched, dark red to olive brown, reaching 15 cm (6 in) tall. Primary branching is alternate, lateral branches are comblike (pectinate), and branch tips are forcipate. Branches are covered with a cortex, and the holdfast is rhizoidal.

Habitat This perennial occurs on rock (occasionally on other algae, sometimes in tide pools) in the mid to low intertidal of semi-exposed habitats.

Similar to *Ceramium pacificum*.

Bleached brunette *Cryptosiphonia woodii*

Coarse sea lace *Microcladia borealis*

Graceful black pine
Neorhodomela aculeata (Perestenko) Masuda

5 cm

Former name *Neorhodomela larix* subsp. *aculeata*

Class Florideophyceae

Order Ceramiales

Family Rhodomelaceae

North Pacific distribution Bering Sea and Aleutian Islands, Alaska, to southern Vancouver Island; Korea; Japan; Russia.

Description Thallus is coarse, reddish black to yellowish brown, reaching at least 25 cm (10 in) tall. Main axes have abundant radially arranged short determinate branches; longer branches are of indeterminate length and arise in the axils of these determinate branches.

Habitat This perennial is found on rocks in the mid to low intertidal of semi-exposed habitats.

Similar to *Neorhodomela larix, N. oregona, Odonthalia floccosa.*

Black pine
Neorhodomela larix (Turner) Masuda

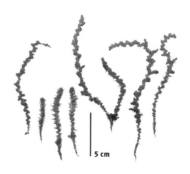

5 cm

Former names *Fucus larix, Fuscaria larix, Rhodomela larix*

Class Florideophyceae

Order Ceramiales

Family Rhodomelaceae

North Pacific distribution Bering Sea and Aleutian Islands, Alaska, to Baja California, Mexico; Japan; Russia.

Description Thallus is stout, black to brownish black, reaching 30 cm (12 in) tall. The main axis has stout, unbranched determinate branches whorled around it like a bottlebrush; indeterminate branches are rare.

Habitat This tough perennial forms mats on rocks in the low intertidal of semi-exposed habitats.

Similar to *Neorhodomela aculeata, N. oregona.*

Graceful black pine *Neorhodomela aculeata*

Black pine *Neorhodomela larix*

Oregon pine

Neorhodomela oregona (Doty) Masuda

Former name *Odonthalia oregona*

Class Florideophyceae

Order Ceramiales

Family Rhodomelaceae

North Pacific distribution Bering Sea and Aleutian Islands, Alaska, to Sonoma County, California; Japan; Russia.

Description Thallus is coarse, reddish brown to black, growing to 17 cm (7 in) tall. Branching of main axis is primarily indeterminate, with slender, terete, radially arranged branches. Thallus is attached by a discoidal holdfast.

Habitat This resilient perennial is found on rocks often in tide pools in the mid intertidal of semi-protected to protected habitats.

Similar to *Neorhodomela aculeata*, *N. larix*, *Cryptosiphonia woodii*, *Odonthalia floccosa* f. *comosa**.

Sea brush

Odonthalia floccosa (Esper) Falkenberg

Former names *Fucus floccosus*, *Fuscaria floccosa*, *Lophura floccosa*, *Rhodomela floccosa*

Class Florideophyceae

Order Ceramiales

Family Rhodomelaceae

North Pacific distribution Bering Sea and Aleutian Islands, Alaska, to northern Washington.

Description Thallus is dark red to brownish black (tips sometimes bleaching blond), growing to 40 cm (16 in) tall. Branching is profuse and alternate, with branches cylindrical to somewhat flattened basally, arranged in two rows on opposite sides of the axis (distichous branching). Tertiary branches bear clusters of short, pointed branchlets. Holdfast is discoidal.

Habitat This perennial is found on rock in the low intertidal of semi-exposed and semi-protected habitats.

Similar to *Neorhodomela* spp., *Odonthalia floccosa* f. *comosa**.

Oregon pine   *Neorhodomela oregona*

Sea brush   *Odonthalia floccosa*

Sea fern
Neoptilota asplenioides (Esper) Kylin ex
Scagel, Garbary, Golden et M.W. Hawkes

Former names *Fucus asplenioides, Plumaria asplenioides, Ptilota asplenioides*

Class Florideophyceae
Order Ceramiales
Family Wrangeliaceae

5 cm

North Pacific distribution Bering Sea and Aleutian Islands, Alaska, to northern Washington; Japan; Russia.

Description Thallus is bright to dark red, shiny, coarsely branched, fern-like, reaching 40 cm (15 in) tall with a tough discoidal holdfast. Ultimate branchlets are flattened, in opposite pairs, with one branch remaining short, unbranched, with serrate margins. The opposite branch is initially shorter but has the potential to become a long, indeterminate branch or to produce sporangia.

Habitat This perennial is found on rock or on larger algae in the low intertidal to shallow subtidal of semi-exposed habitats.

Similar to *Neoptilota hypnoides*† lacks serrated margins, *Ptilota serrata*

Northern sea fern
Ptilota serrata Kützing

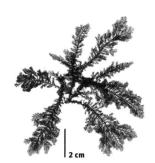

Former name *Ptilota pectinata*

Class Florideophyceae
Order Ceramiales
Family Wrangeliaceae

North Pacific distribution Bering Sea and Aleutian Islands to Oregon; Korea; Japan; Russia.

2 cm

Description Thallus is dark red, dull, finely branched, reaching 25 cm (9 in) tall. Branching is in opposite pairs, with both branchlets having the potential to elongate, branch, and produce reproductive structures, although usually one of a pair develops ahead of the other. Indeterminate branches often develop in the axils of branchlets.

Habitat This perennial is found on rock, other algae, or even animals in the low intertidal to subtidal of semi-protected to semi-exposed habitats.

Similar to *Neoptilota asplenioides*.

Sea fern   *Neoptilota asplenioides*

Northern sea fern   *Ptilota serrata*

Seagrass laver

Smithora naiadum (C.L. Anderson) Hollenberg

> **Former names** *Porphyra naiadum,*
> *Membranella nitens*
>
> **Class** Compsopogonophyceae
> **Order** Erythropeltidales
> **Family** Erythrotrichiaceae
>
> **North Pacific distribution** Alaska Peninsula,
> Alaska, to Baja California, Mexico.

2 cm

Eelgrass host

Description Thalli are small, thin, roundish to elongate, purplish pink blades to 5 cm (2 in) tall; they arise from cushion-like bases along the margins of seagrass blades.

Habitat This species is epiphytic on seagrasses in the low intertidal and upper subtidal.

Similar to *Pyropia gardneri* occurs along the margins of *Laminaria* blades.

Dark laver

Fuscifolium papenfussii (V. Krishnamurthy) S.C. Lindstrom
and Fuscifolium tasa (Yendo) S.C. Lindstrom

> **Former names** *Porphyra papenfussii, Porphyra
> tasa*
>
> **Class** Bangiophyceae
> **Order** Bangiales
> **Family** Bangiaceae
>
> **North Pacific distributions** Kodiak archipelago,
> Alaska, to Oregon (*Fuscifolium papenfussii*) and
> Aleutian Islands, Alaska; Russia (*Fuscifolium tasa*).

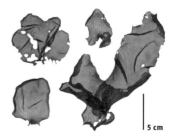

5 cm

Description Thallus is a dark brown (occasionally green) blade, two cell layers thick, nearly circular to irregular in outline, reaching 60 cm (24 in) in diameter. Male and female reproductive cells are on separate thalli or on different lobes of the same thallus.

Habitat These two species are annuals; they occur in the mid intertidal of semi-protected to exposed habitats.

Similar to *Wildemania norrisii**.

Black Seaweed

Pyropia abbottiae (V. Krishnamurthy) S.C. Lindstrom

5 cm

Former name *Porphyra abbottiae*

Class Bangiophyceae

Order Bangiales

Family Bangiaceae

North Pacific distribution Sanak Island, Alaska, to northern California.

Description Thallus is a green blade, to ~50 cm (20 in) long, one cell layer thick and often deeply ruffled along the margin, especially in lower half. The margin becomes bright red when female cells are fertilized; male cells are in diamond-shaped streaks extending from near margin toward center of blade.

Habitat This species is found on lower mid intertidal rock in spring and early summer, often on barnacles, on exposed or partially exposed shores.

Similar to *Pyropia fallax* has paler female reproductive patches; *Wildemania norrisii** is thicker, less ruffled; *Pyropia perforata** is rounder and more uniform in color.

Black Seaweed *Pyropia abbottiae*

Summer laver

Boreophyllum aestivale (S.C. Lindstrom & Fredericq) S.C. Lindstrom

5 cm

Former name *Porphyra aestivalis;* **misidentified as** *P. umbilicalis*

Class Bangiophyceae

Order Bangiales

Family Bangiaceae

North Pacific distribution Bering Sea and Aleutian Islands to Haida Gwaii, British Columbia

Description This is one of the most common species of foliose Bangiales in Alaska. Thallus is a monostromatic blade that can vary in color from pale pink to grayish purple to dark green and in shape from circular to elongate. When reproductive, male and female cells are segregated on different halves of the thallus.

Habitat This ephemeral occurs on rock in summer in the mid to low intertidal of semi-protected to semi-exposed habitats.

Similar to *Pyropia kurogii*[†], a spring species, is usually smaller, more ovate, and a paler color; *Pyropia fucicola* and *P. perforata** have sexual cells intermixed on their blades.

Red cellophane

Wildemania amplissima (Kjellman) Foslie

2 cm

Former names *Wildemania cuneiformis, Porphyra cuneiformis, P. miniata* f. *cuneiformis*

Class Bangiophyceae

Order Bangiales

Family Bangiaceae

North Pacific distribution Aleutian Islands, Alaska, to Monterey Peninsula, California; Russia.

Description Thallus is light pink, variable in shape, and can reach more than 100 cm (39 in) long. It is very thin, with two cell layers (distromatic). The margin of the blade often appears filmy because of scattered reproductive cells.

Habitat This species is often found on clamshells on sandy beaches at low tide in spring and early summer; it can also grow on rock.

Similar to *Wildemania variegata**, another distromatic species, is thicker, and the blade is sectored into separate male and female "halves."

Summer laver *Boreophyllum aestivale*

Red cellophane *Wildemania amplissima*

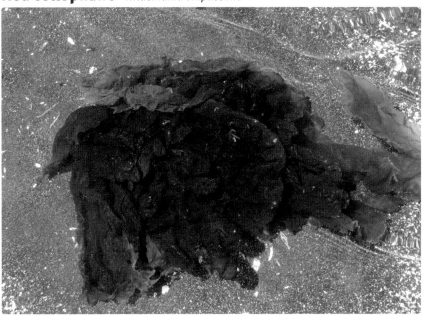

131

False laver

Pyropia fallax (S.C. Lindstrom et K.M.Cole) S.C. Lindstrom

5 cm

Former name *Porphyra fallax*

Class Bangiophyceae
Order Bangiales
Family Bangiaceae

North Pacific distribution Aleutian Islands, Alaska, to northern Washington.

Description This may be the most common species of *Pyropia* in Alaska. Thallus is a reddish-brown blade, to ~50 cm (20 in) long, elongate, with a greenish center, one cell layer thick, and often ruffled along the margin. The margin becomes pale red when female cells are fertilized; male cells are in whitish patches or streaks.

Habitat High to lower mid intertidal rock from winter to early summer, from protected to exposed shores, often associated with sand.

Similar to *Pyropia abbottiae* has darker red female reproductive patches; *Pyropia perforata** is rounder and more uniform in color.

Rockweed laver

Pyropia fucicola (V. Krishnamurthy) S.C. Lindstrom

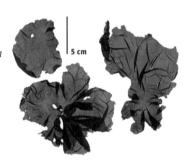

5 cm

Former names *Porphyra fucicola, P. maculosa*

Class Bangiophyceae
Order Bangiales
Family Bangiaceae

North Pacific distribution Aleutian Islands, Alaska, to California.

Description Thalli of nearly circular blades reach ~15 cm (6 in) in diameter, color uniform brown (center occasionally grayish with reddish margin), one cell layer and appearing thin. Reproductive cells are occasionally evident as lightly pigmented, diamond-shaped patches around blade margin.

Habitat This species is mostly in the mid intertidal although it can extend higher or lower, and can grow on rocks, on algae (often on *Fucus* or *Endocladia*), or on animals (barnacles).

Similar to *Pyropia perforata** is thicker.

False laver *Pyropia fallax*

Rockweed laver *Pyropia fucicola*

Kelp laver

Pyropia gardneri (G.M. Smith et Hollenberg) S.C. Lindstrom

Former names *Porphyra gardneri, Porphyrella gardneri*

Class Bangiophyceae

Order Bangiales

Family Bangiaceae

North Pacific distribution Aleutian Islands, Alaska, to Baja California, Mexico; Commander Islands, Russia.

2 cm

Description Thallus is somewhat oval, to 12 cm (5 in) long, reddish pink, one cell layer thick, with the margin slightly ruffled to somewhat ragged. Sexes are intermixed.

Habitat This species grows in large numbers along the edges of blades of *Laminaria* and sometimes other kelps in the low intertidal and subtidal of semi-exposed and exposed habitats.

Similar to *Wildemania variegata*, another common epiphyte on kelps, is larger and has a blade sectored into separate male and female "halves."

Bull kelp laver

Pyropia nereocystis (C.L. Anderson) S.C. Lindstrom

Former names *Porphyra nereocystis, Pyropia californica*

Class Bangiophyceae

Order Bangiales

Family Bangiaceae

North Pacific distribution Eastern Aleutian Islands (Umnak Island), Alaska, to San Luis Obispo County, California.

5 cm

Description Thallus is a reddish pink strap-shaped blade, one cell layer thick, that often reaches 100 cm (39 in) or more in length and 30 cm (12 in) broad. Spermatangia and zygotosporangia occur in wide marginal or submarginal bands or streaks.

Habitat This species grows on the stipe of the bull kelp, *Nereocystis luetkeana*, and rarely on other hosts; it is always submerged.

Similar to *Wildemania amplissima* occasionally also grows epiphytically on *Nereocystis*.

Kelp laver *Pyropia gardneri*

Bull kelp laver *Pyropia nereocystis*

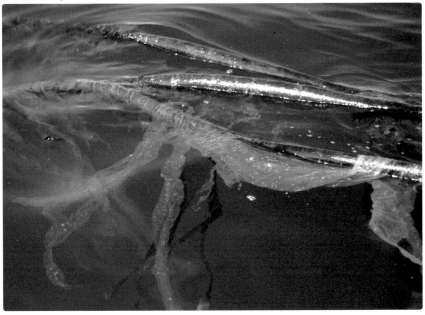

Long laver
Pyropia **sp.** (undescribed)

Misidentified as *Porphyra pseudolinearis*

Class Bangiophyceae
Order Bangiales
Family Bangiaceae

North Pacific distribution Bering Sea and Aleutian Islands to northern Southeast Alaska; Russia.

5 cm

Description Thallus is a linear blade, one cell layer thick, reaching about 40 cm (16 in) long and 2 cm (0.75 in) wide, usually reddish pink or reddish brown. Male cells are in whitish margins; fertilized female cells are in hieroglyph-like streaks across distal ends of separate female plants.

Habitat This species occurs on low intertidal rock in spring to early summer. In western Aleutians, this species is found in the high to mid intertidal, where it is more brownish in color.

Olive green winter laver
Pyropia pseudolanceolata (V. Krishnamurthy) S.C. Lindstrom

Former name *Porphyra pseudolanceolata*

Class Bangiophyceae
Order Bangiales
Family Bangiaceae

North Pacific distribution Aleutian Islands, Alaska, to Del Norte County, California.

5 cm

Description Thallus is an olive green blade, to ~30 cm (12 in) long but usually much shorter, one cell layer thick; lanceolate when young, becoming rounder near the base with age. Male cells are in whitish margins; fertilized female cells are in hieroglyph-like streaks across distal ends of separate female plants.

Habitat This species is restricted to high intertidal bedrock on exposed coasts in winter, surviving into spring or even summer at colder sites.

Similar to *Pyropia lanceolata*[†], which looks identical, co-occurs with this species in Sitka Sound.

Long laver *Pyropia* sp.

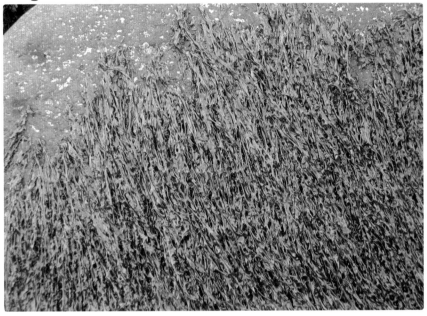

Olive green winter laver *Pyropia pseudolanceolata*

Turkish washcloth
Mastocarpus alaskensis S.C. Lindstrom, Hughey et Martone

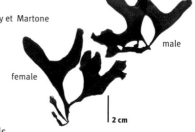

female

male

2 cm

Misidentified as *Mastocarpus papillatus*

Class Florideophyceae
Order Gigartinales
Family Phyllophoraceae

North Pacific distribution Aleutian Islands, Alaska, to northern California; Russia.

Description Thallus is a branched blade, reddish brown (almost black) to yellowish brown, tough, reaching 15 cm (6 in) tall; branching dichotomous to irregular. This perennial species arises from a *Petrocelis*-like base (crust-like); female thalli have distinct bumps (papillae), like a rough washcloth.

Habitat One of our most common seaweeds, growing on rocks from the high to mid intertidal of semi-protected to semi-exposed habitats.

Similar to *Mastocarpus latissimus*[†] and *M. intermedius*[†], which occur in low intertidal habitats.

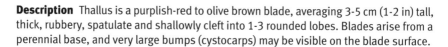

Iridescent horn-of-plenty
Mazzaella parksii (Setchell et N.L. Gardner)
Hughey, P.C. Silva et Hommersand

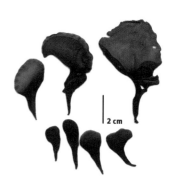

2 cm

Former name *Iridophycus parksii*

Misidentified as *Iridaea cornucopiae*, *Mazzaella cornucopiae*

Class Florideophyceae
Order Gigartinales
Family Gigartinaceae

North Pacific distribution Aleutian Islands, Alaska, to Mendocino County, California; Russia.

Description Thallus is a purplish-red to olive brown blade, averaging 3-5 cm (1-2 in) tall, thick, rubbery, spatulate and shallowly cleft into 1-3 rounded lobes. Blades arise from a perennial base, and very large bumps (cystocarps) may be visible on the blade surface.

Habitat This species forms dense clusters or carpets on rock in the high intertidal of semi-exposed to exposed coastlines.

Similar to Male *Mastocarpus alaskensis* has a similar shape and color but is slightly more cartilaginous.

138

Turkish washcloth *Mastocarpus alaskensis*

Iridescent horn-of-plenty *Mazzaella parksii*

Northern mazza weed

Mazzaella phyllocarpa (Postels et Ruprecht) Perestenko

tetrasporic

2 cm

cystocarpic

Former names *Iridaea lilacina, I. furcata;*
misidentified as *Iridaea heterocarpa*

Class Florideophyceae

Order Gigartinales

Family Gigartinaceae

North Pacific distribution Bering Sea and
Aleutian Islands to Southeast Alaska; Russia.

Description Thallus is usually burgundy red, somewhat rubbery, not iridescent,
to 15 cm (6 in) tall and nearly as wide. Blades are deeply cleft into irregular, often
pointed lobes. Reproductive blades have large cystocarps (4 mm diameter) bulging
from the blade surface.

Habitat This species grows on rock in the low intertidal, often in tide pools, of semi-
protected and semi-exposed habitats; it also occurs subtidally.

Similar to *Mazzaella oregona*[†], *M. parvula*[†], *M. parksii.*

Frilly red ribbon

Palmaria callophylloides M.W. Hawkes et Scagel

Misidentified as *Palmaria palmata*
f. *sarniensis, Devaleraea ramentacea*

Class Florideophyceae

Order Palmariales

Family Palmariacae

2 cm

North Pacific distribution Aleutian Islands,
Alaska, to northern British Columbia; Russia.

Description Thallus is crisp, shiny, deep red to yellowish pink, reaching 10-15 cm
(4-10 in) tall. The thallus is narrow, flattened, repeatedly dichotomously branched,
occasionally palmate, tapering to a discoidal holdfast. Some thalli become hollow
and resemble the North Atlantic species *Devaleraea ramentacea.*

Habitat This annual occurs on rock in the high to mid, sometimes low,
intertidal (generally above *Palmaria hecatensis* and *P. mollis*, if present) of semi-
exposed habitats.

Similar to *Palmaria mollis, Callophyllis* spp.*

Northern mazza weed *Mazzaella phyllocarpa*

Frilly red ribbon *Palmaria callophylloides*

Stiff red ribbon
Palmaria hecatensis M.W. Hawkes

5 cm

Misidentified as *Rhodymenia palmata*
f. *palmata*, *Palmaria palmata*

Class Florideophyceae
Order Palmariales
Family Palmariaceae

North Pacific distribution Aleutian Islands,
Alaska, to northern California; Russia.

Description Thallus is leathery, somewhat shiny, deep red to maroon, to at least 20 cm (8 in) tall. The blade is strap-like, unbranched or with 1 or 2 lobes with rounded tips, tapering to a discoidal holdfast.

Habitat This annual is found on rock in the mid to low intertidal (usually above *P. mollis*) of semi-exposed habitats. This species is edible, a good source of vitamins and minerals, and similar to the Atlantic species *Palmaria palmata* (dulse).

Similar to *Palmaria mollis* is thinner and more glove-shaped than the mitten-shape of *P. hecatensis*.

Red ribbon
Palmaria mollis (Setchell et N.L. Gardner) van der Meer et C.J. Bird

5 cm

Former names *Rhodymenia palmata* f. *mollis*,
Palmaria palmata f. *mollis*

Class Florideophyceae
Order Palmariales
Family Palmariaceae

North Pacific distribution Bering Sea and Aleutian Islands, Alaska, to San Luis Obispo County, California; Russia.

Description Thallus is crisp, somewhat dull, medium red to yellowish pink, reaching 30 cm (12 in) or taller. The blade is palmate, with irregular lobes and dichotomies, wedge-shaped at base, tapering to a discoidal holdfast. This species is edible and a good source of vitamins and minerals.

Habitat This species is biennial, with bladelets proliferating from the previous years' stub; it occurs on rock in the mid to low intertidal and subtidal of semi-protected to semi-exposed habitats.

Similar to *Palmaria* spp., *Sparlingia pertusa*.

Stiff red ribbon *Palmaria hecatensis*

Red ribbon *Palmaria mollis*

Red eyelet silk

Sparlingia pertusa (Postels et Ruprecht) G.W. Saunders, I.M. Strachan et Kraft

Former names *Porphyra pertusa,*
Rhodymenia pertusa, R. stipitata

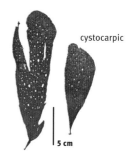

cystocarpic

5 cm

Class Florideophyceae

Order Rhodymeniales

Family Rhodymeniaceae

North Pacific distribution Bering Sea and
Aleutian Islands, Alaska, to Oregon; Korea;
Japan; Russia.

Description Thallus is rose red (bleaching to yellow later in season), somewhat crisp, reaching 60 cm (24 in) tall and 20 cm (8 in) wide. The blade is usually undivided (entire), rounded at the top, perforated with small holes, tapering rapidly to a stipe (variable length), and attached to a small discoidal holdfast. Cystocarps occur as small dark bumps on blade surface.

Habitat This annual is found on rock in the low intertidal and subtidal (to at least 18 m depth) of semi-exposed habitats.

Similar to *Palmaria mollis.*

Red sea cabbage

Turnerella mertensiana (Postels et Ruprecht) F. Schmitz

Former names *Iridaea mertensiana, I. punicea*

5 cm

Class Florideophyceae

Order Gigartinales

Family Furcellariaceae

North Pacific distribution Bering Sea and
Aleutian Islands, Alaska, to northern Washington;
Japan; Russia.

Description Thallus is a dark red blade. It lacks a stipe and attaches to the substrate by a small discoidal holdfast. Young blades are frequently undivided (entire) and nearly round, reaching at least 30 cm (12 in) in diameter, but older blades split and become tattered, irregular in shape, and very thick. The large, white "gland cells" in the cortex can be seen with the aid of a hand lens.

Habitat This perennial occurs on rock in the low intertidal to subtidal of semi-protected to semi-exposed shores.

Similar to *Opuntiella.*

Red eyelet silk *Sparlingia pertusa*

Red sea cabbage *Turnerella mertensiana*

Winged rib

Cumathamnion decipiens (J. Agardh) M.J. Wynne et G.W. Saunders

Former name *Delesseria decipiens, Apoglossum decipiens*

Class Florideophyceae

Order Ceramiales

Family Delesseriaceae

North Pacific distribution Kodiak archipelago, Alaska, to San Luis Obispo County, California.

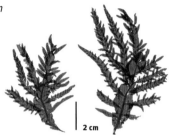

2 cm

Description Thallus is rose red to light pink, reaching 25 cm (10 in) or more in height with a prominent midrib throughout with a delicate blade on either side of the midrib. Alternate branching along the midrib produces branches of the same morphology as the main axis, to several orders. Blade narrows basally to a short stipe and small discoidal holdfast.

Habitat This spring ephemeral occurs on rock in the low intertidal and subtidal (to 18 m) of semi-protected to semi-exposed habitats.

Similar to *Membranoptera dimorpha*[†].

Common sea oak

Phycodrys fimbriata (Kuntze) Kylin

Former names *Membranoptera fimbriata, Phycodrys riggii, P. serratiloba*

Class Florideophyceae

Order Ceramiales

Family Delesseriaceae

North Pacific distribution Arctic Ocean, Bering Sea and Aleutian Islands, Alaska, to northern British Columbia; Commander Islands, Russia.

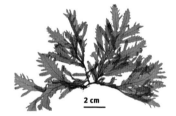

2 cm

Description Thallus is rose red to dusky pink, delicate, mostly under 10 cm (4 in) tall with thin, narrow blades (to 0.6 cm wide) with conspicuous midrib, less conspicuous paired lateral veins, and irregular, narrow teeth along margins that can develop into lateral branches. Holdfast is discoidal or of ribbonlike branches similar to lateral branches.

Habitat This perennial is found on rock in the low intertidal of semi-protected to semi-exposed habitats. (High intertidal in photo is not the natural habitat for this species.)

Similar to *Mikamiella ruprechtiana, Tokidadendron bullatum.*

Winged rib *Cumathamnion decipiens*

Common sea oak *Phycodrys fimbriata*

Mikami's sea oak
Mikamiella ruprechtiana (Zinova) M.J. Wynne

5 cm

Former name *Hypophyllum ruprechtianum*

Class Florideophyceae

Order Ceramiales

Family Delesseriaceae

North Pacific distribution Bering Sea and Aleutian Islands to Southeast Alaska; Russia.

Description Thallus is dark red to dusky pink, crisp, shiny, reaching 40 cm (16 in) tall. Blades are oval to elongate, with midrib and conspicuous, branched lateral veins; margins are undulate, sometimes with spine-like teeth. Holdfast is discoidal or of ribbonlike branches. Reproductive structures are on bladelets along midrib or veins.

Habitat This perennial is usually found in the subtidal zone (0-20 m) on rock or other algae in semi-exposed to exposed habitats.

Similar to *Congregatocarpus kurilensis*[†] and *Yendonia crassifolia*[†] differ in anatomical and reproductive features and are much less common.

Northern sea oak
Tokidadendron bullatum (N.L. Gardner) M.J. Wynne

2 cm

Former names *Tokidadendron ambigua*, *Phycodrys ambigua*, *Phycodrys bullata*, *Pseudophycodrys rainosukei*

Class Florideophyceae

Order Ceramiales

Family Delesseriaceae

North Pacific distribution Aleutian Islands, Alaska, to Haida Gwaii, British Columbia; northern Japan; Russia.

Description Thallus is dark red to dusky pink, somewhat crisp, usually 12 cm (5 in) or less in height and up to 5 cm (2 in), wide with smooth, undulating margins, cartilaginous midrib, and opposite veins. Cystocarps develop directly on midrib and veins whereas tetrasporangia develop over the blade. Blades disintegrate after reproduction in spring, leaving only the perennial midrib until new blades proliferate from it the following spring.

Habitat This species is found on rock in the low intertidal to shallow subtidal of semi-protected to semi-exposed habitats.

Similar to *Congregatocarpus kurilensis*[†].

Mikami's sea oak *Mikamiella ruprechtiana*

Northern sea oak *Tokidadendron bullatum*

Red Seaweeds

Cracked saucer
Constantinea subulifera Setchell

5 cm

Class Florideophyceae

Order Gigartinales

Family Dumontiaceae

North Pacific distribution Aleutian Islands, Alaska, to northern Washington; Japan; Russia.

Description Thallus is dark red, saucer-shaped; blades frequently lacerated, attached in the middle of their lower side to a branched, cylindrical stipe. Thallus grows up to 20 cm (10 in) tall overall with blades to 30 cm (12 in) in diameter. Blades have conspicuous veins on their underside, where tetrasporangial sori develop. This perennial grows a new blade each winter at the end of the stipe that protrudes through the center of the previous year's blade beginning in late spring.

Habitat This species is found on rock in the low intertidal to shallow subtidal of semi-protected to semi-exposed habitats. (Photo does not show the natural habitat for this species.)

Similar to *Constantinea rosa-marina.*

Cup and saucer
Constantinea rosa-marina (S.G. Gmelin) Postels et Ruprecht

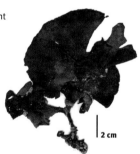

2 cm

Former name *Fucus rosa-marina*

Class Florideophyceae

Order Gigartinales

Family Dumontiaceae

North Pacific distribution Bering Sea and Aleutian Islands to Southeast Alaska; Japan; Russia.

Description Thallus is dark red, saucer-shaped, with usually entire (not lacerated) blades less than 15 cm (6 in) diameter, attached in the middle of their lower side to a branched, cylindrical stipe. Veins are inconspicuous. Thallus grows up to ~15 cm (6 in) tall. The stipe never protrudes. New blades develop each winter from the center of the previous year's blade, and the stipe between the new and old blade elongates as the new blade expands.

Habitat This perennial occurs on rock, mostly in the subtidal zone of semi-protected to semi-exposed habitats.

Similar to *C. simplex*[†] does not undergo stipe elongation; *Constantinea subulifera.*

Cracked saucer *Constantinea subulifera*

Cup and saucer *Constantinea rosa-marina*

Rubber threads
Nemalion elminthoides (Velley) Batters

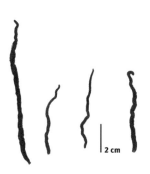

Former names *Fucus elminthoides,
Nemalion helminthoides, N. lubricum*

Class Florideophyceae
Order Nemaliales
Family Liagoraceae

North Pacific distribution Afognak Island,
Alaska, to Baja California, Mexico; Japan.

Description Thallus is reddish brown, reaching 20 cm (8 in) tall, attached by a cushion-like holdfast. This solid but soft, rubbery cord usually grows in clumps and may be irregularly branched.

Habitat This is a summer annual, which grows on barnacles or rock in the high to mid intertidal of semi-exposed to exposed habitats.

Similar to Commonly misidentified as a wormlike invertebrate.

Red opuntia
Opuntiella californica (Farlow) Kylin

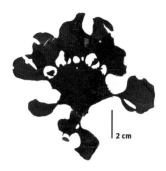

Former names *Kallymenia californica,
Cruoria profunda*

Class Florideophyceae
Order Gigartinales
Family Furcellariaceae

North Pacific distribution Bering Sea and
Aleutian Islands, Alaska, to Baja California,
Mexico.

Description Thallus is dark red, thick, reaching 20 cm (8 in) tall and 30 cm (12 in) wide, with the central blade bearing numerous additional blades from its margin, repeated to several orders (similar to prickly pear cactus), with distinct stipe and fleshy discoidal holdfast. A faint midrib may be evident near the base of some blades. The alternate reproductive phase (tetrasporophyte) is crustose.

Habitat This perennial is found on rock in the low intertidal and subtidal (to 20 m) of semi-protected to exposed habitats.

Similar to *Turnerella*.

152

Rubber threads *Nemalion elminthoides*

Red opuntia *Opuntiella californica*

Black sea-hair
Bangia spp.

North Pacific distribution Throughout the area.

Description Thallus is an unbranched, narrow, hair-like filament of dark red cells, tapering to a base just one cell wide, with cells forming rhizoidal extensions that help attach the filament to the substrate. Filaments are 10 cm (4 in) long and 0.15 mm (0.006 in) diameter. One species is found on high intertidal rock in spring; a different species occurs on mid intertidal rock in summer. Filaments dry as dark skeins flat against the rock.

2 cm

Winged coral seaweed
Bossiella spp.

North Pacific distribution Kodiak archipelago, Alaska, to Baja California, Mexico.

Description Thallus is pink, articulated, calcareous, with flattened, wing nut–shaped segments. Some species reach 12 cm (5 in) tall, but most species are much shorter. Branching is pinnate, to several orders, or repeatedly dichotomous, mostly in one plane. Species in this genus are perennial and occur on rock in the low intertidal and subtidal of semi-protected to exposed habitats.

1 cm

Red sea fan
Callophyllis spp.

North Pacific distribution Throughout the area (except the Arctic Ocean).

Description Thallus is red, flattened, fan-shaped, more or less dichotomously branched, with branch segments narrow or wide and short or long (depending on species). Species are subtidal (rarely low intertidal); some occur on rock, others are epiphytic or even epizoic. Most appear to be perennial.

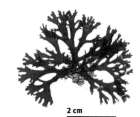

2 cm

Turkish towel
Chondracanthus exasperatus
(Harvey et Bailey) Hughey

North Pacific distribution Sitka Sound, Alaska, to Baja California, Mexico.

Description Thallus is a thick (somewhat rubbery), elongate, undivided, purplish to pale red blade, reaching 30 cm (12 in) tall, with short, spiny papillae covering the blade surface. Blades arise as elongate papillae-like projections from a discoidal holdfast up to 1 cm (0.4 in) in diameter. This perennial grows on rock in the low intertidal and upper subtidal of semi-protected to semi-exposed habitats.

5 cm

Common coral seaweed
Corallina sp.

North Pacific distribution Alaska Peninsula, Alaska, to Baja California, Mexico.

Description Thallus is pink, articulated, calcareous, with cylindrical segments, reaching 10 cm (4 in) tall. Branching is pinnate, to several orders, lying in one plane, usually with space between branches. This perennial species occurs on rock in the low intertidal and subtidal of semi-protected to exposed habitats.

1 cm

Hidden rib
Cryptopleura ruprechtiana (J. Agardh) Kylin

North Pacific distribution Kodiak archipelago, Alaska, to Baja California, Mexico.

Description Thallus is a papery thin, rose red, fan-shaped blade with fine veins radiating from near the base. The blade is dissected into numerous lobes, which can be fringed with tiny bladelets. Blades can reach 20 cm (8 in) or more in height and are often broader than tall. This perennial occurs on rock in the low intertidal to subtidal in semi-protected to semi-exposed habitats.

5 cm

Delicate northern sea fan
Euthora cristata (C. Agardh) J. Agardh

North Pacific distribution Bering Sea and Aleutian Islands, Alaska, to northern Washington; Japan; Russia.

Description Thallus is rose red, branched, reaching 12 cm (5 in) tall but usually shorter. The main axis is 5 mm (0.2 in) or less wide, and the highly subdivided branches become narrower toward their tips. This species grows on a variety of hosts (rock, other algae, animals) in the low intertidal and subtidal of semi-protected to exposed habitats.

1 cm

Farlow's seaweed
Farlowia mollis (Harvey et Bailey) Farlow et Setchell

North Pacific distribution Prince William Sound, Alaska, to Baja California, Mexico; Japan; Russia.

Description Thallus is medium to dark red, soft and slippery, narrow and strap-like, to 20 cm (8 in) tall and 1.5 cm (0.6 in) wide but usually much shorter, branched or unbranched, with fringe-like laterals. This species has a faint midrib and veins, which are not always evident. It occurs on low intertidal rock or in mid tide pools in exposed to semi-protected habitats of the outer coast.

2 cm

Hommersand's seaweed
Hommersandia maximicarpa
G.I. Hansen et S.C. Lindstrom

North Pacific distribution Bering Sea and Aleutian Islands, Alaska, to Vancouver Island, British Columbia.

Description Thallus is a deep red, often with marginal bladelets, tapering to a short stipe and small, discoidal holdfast. Thallus can reach 23 cm (9 in) tall and 35 cm (14 in) wide but is usually <10 cm (4 in). This perennial grows on rock, shell, other algae, and debris in the subtidal of protected to exposed habitats.

2 cm

Sea fern fringe
Hymenena ruthenica (Postels et Ruprecht) Zinova

North Pacific distribution Bering Sea and Aleutian Islands to Kodiak archipelago, Alaska; Russia.

Description Thallus is a thin, papery blade of deeply lacerated, wedge-shaped segments to at least 20 cm (8 in) in height and 3 cm (1.2 in) wide. Blades are frequently fertile, with either cystocarpic bumps or small, elliptical tetrasporangial sori. This species is often epiphytic on *Neoptilota asplenioides* and other algae in the low intertidal and subtidal of semi-exposed habitats.

5 cm

Russian red blade
Kallymeniopsis spp.

North Pacific distribution Bering Sea and Aleutian Islands, Alaska, to northern California; Russia.

Description Thallus is a brownish red to dark red blade, sometimes entire but more frequently split nearly to base of blade, which can reach 30 cm (12 in) tall. Blade surface is smooth or with tiny projections (verrucose), making the surface feel like sandpaper. The base of the stipe, if present, is often nearly colorless; holdfast is small, discoidal. Species are probably perennial; they are mostly subtidal in a variety of habitats.

5 cm

Narrow Turkish washcloth
Mastocarpus rigidus (J. Agardh) S.C. Lindstrom, Hughey et Martone

North Pacific distribution Aleutian Islands, Alaska, to San Luis Obispo County, California.

Description Thallus is reddish brown to almost black, tough, narrow, flattened, to 10 cm (4 in) tall, sometimes flaring into a blade at the distal end, which is usually covered with papillae. Like Turkish washcloth, this species alternates with a diploid tar spot crust. It grows in clusters on rock in the mid intertidal of semi-exposed and exposed habitats.

5 cm

157

Splendid iridescent seaweed
Mazzaella splendens (Setchell et N.L. Gardner) Fredericq

North Pacific distribution Northern Southeast Alaska, to Baja California, Mexico.

Description Thallus is an undivided, cordate to lanceolate blade, to 30 cm (12 in) or taller, sometimes lobed, very rubbery, and usually an iridescent brownish or purplish red. Northern specimens are smaller than those found from British Columbia south. This annual (with perennial crustose base) grows on rock in the low intertidal of semi-protected to exposed habitats.

5 cm

Bering membrane wing
Membranoptera spinulosa (Ruprecht) Kuntze

North Pacific distribution Bering Sea and Aleutian Islands to Southeast Alaska; Japan; Russia.

Description Thallus is pale red, to 7 cm (3 in) tall, with a midrib running the length of the thin, narrow, branched blades, and with microscopic lateral veins. Margins smooth or toothed (denticulate). Thallus is attached to the substrate, which can be rock, other algae, or animals, by a small discoidal holdfast. This species is an annual; it occurs on rock in the low intertidal (if higher, in tide pools) and subtidal in semi-protected to semi-exposed habitats.

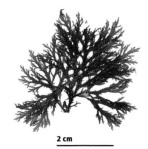

2 cm

Northern red blade
Neodilsea borealis (I.A. Abbott) S.C. Lindstrom

North Pacific distribution Alaska Peninsula, Alaska, to northern Washington.

Description Thallus is a dark red blade bleaching to yellow, entire, often somewhat wrinkled, tapering to a short, slender stipe and minute discoidal holdfast. It is usually less than 30 cm (12 in) tall but can attain 1 m (39 in). Although it can be somewhat shiny in appearance, it is never slippery, and veins and midrib are lacking. This uncommon species is a biennial; it grows on pebbles in soft sediment in the extreme low intertidal and upper subtidal of protected or semi-protected habitats.

5 cm

Lesser sea brush
Odonthalia floccosa f. *comosa*
Setchell et N.L. Gardner

> **North Pacific distribution** Aleutian Islands, Alaska, to Point Conception, California; Russia.

Description Thallus is dark brown to black, to ~20 cm (8 in) tall, main axis cylindrical to slightly compressed, with numerous short branchlets clustered along the axis and on indeterminate branches. This alga occurs on mid intertidal bedrock, often forming a band, on semi-protected to exposed shores.

Russian sea brush
Odonthalia setacea (Ruprecht) Perestenko

> **North Pacific distribution** Bering Sea and Aleutian Islands, Alaska, to northern Washington; Russia.

Description Thallus is dark red, profusely branched in a single plane, reaching 30 cm (12 in) or taller. Main axis is narrow, somewhat sinusoidal. Branches often terminate in clustered branchlets. This perennial occurs on rock (occasionally epiphytic) in the low intertidal and subtidal of semi-exposed to exposed habitats.

Crisscross network
Polyneura latissima (Harvey) Kylin

> **North Pacific distribution** Prince William Sound, Alaska, to Baja California, Mexico; Commander Islands, Russia.

Description Thallus is a thin, crinkly, rose-red blade, to 15 cm (6 in) tall and about half as wide. A crisscrossing network of veins permeates the thallus, which often has bumps (cystocarps) and may develop holes. Found in the low intertidal and subtidal on rock in semi-exposed to semi-protected habitats.

159

Norris' laver
Wildemania norrisii (V. Krishnamurthy) S.C. Lindstrom

North Pacific distribution Aleutian Islands, Alaska, to northern California.

Description Thallus is an olive-green, distromatic blade to 30 cm (12 in) long, strap-like or egg-shaped (ovate) and deeply lobed (hood-shaped) around the basal attachment. Male and female reproductive cells occur on separate individuals. This species occurs on bedrock in the mid to high intertidal on semi-protected to fully exposed shores. It was formerly included in *Porphyra schizophylla*[†].

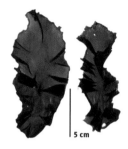
5 cm

Purple laver
Pyropia perforata (J. Agardh) S.C. Lindstrom

North Pacific distribution Kodiak archipelago, Alaska, to Baja California, Mexico.

Description Thallus is a purple (sometimes dark green), broadly expanded blade a single cell layer thick. Sexes are intermixed along the margin of the blade. This species is common from British Columbia south but is less common in Alaska. It occurs in the mid intertidal on rock in semi-protected to semi-exposed habitats.

5 cm

Kjellman's laver
Wildemania variegata (Kjellman) De Toni

North Pacific distribution Bering Sea and Aleutian Islands to Southeast Alaska; Japan; Russia.

Description Thallus is a dusky to pale red, distromatic, wedge-shaped blade that can reach over a meter (39 in) in length although it is usually much smaller. Male and female reproductive cells occur on separate sectors of the blade, which is often somewhat slippery. This species occurs on rock or other algae in the low intertidal to subtidal of semi-exposed to exposed habitats.

5 cm

Bleachweed
Prionitis sternbergii (C. Agardh) J. Agardh

North Pacific distribution Yakutat, Alaska, to Baja California, Mexico.

Description This species smells similar to bleach. Thallus is strap-like, dark reddish brown to almost black, abundantly branched to several orders from a main axis, to 40 cm (16 in) tall. Branches thick, flattened, with many lateral proliferations, at first like small, narrow teeth but enlarging into lanceolate bladelets. This species is perennial and occurs on rock in the low intertidal or in tide pools of semi-protected to exposed habitats.

5 cm

Subtidal tassel
Pterosiphonia hamata E.S. Zinova

North Pacific distribution Bering Sea and Aleutian Islands, Alaska, to northern Washington; Russia.

Description Thallus is fine, profusely branched, dark red to reddish-brown, reaching at least 20 cm (8 in) tall. A microscope is required for accurate identification of the polysiphonous axes, in which 6-7 pericentral cells surround the axial cell. This species is a subtidal perennial that often uses its hooklike branches to wrap around other algae in semi-protected to exposed habitats.

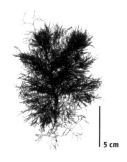

5 cm

Rhodoliths

North Pacific distribution Scattered throughout the area.

Description Thalli are pink, unattached and calcareous: they belong to several different taxa. They are very irregular in shape, often with scattered protuberances and excavations that can harbor a variety of invertebrates, and reaching several centimeters in diameter. These occur in the subtidal in mostly protected habitats such as bays and lagoons.

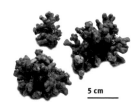

5 cm

161

Slippery red blade
Schizymenia pacifica (Kylin) Kylin

2 cm

North Pacific distribution Aleutian Islands, Alaska, to Baja California, Mexico; Russia.

Description Thallus is a slippery brownish red blade resembling tanned leather in texture. Blades are roundish, often lacerated, with short stipe and small discoidal holdfast. Narrow, elongate gland cells may be visible under a microscope. This annual grows on rock in the low intertidal and subtidal of semi- to fully exposed habitats.

Macmillan's coral seaweed
Johansenia macmillanii (Yendo) K. Hind et G.W. Saunders

2 cm

North Pacific distribution Kodiak archipelago, Alaska, to Channel Islands, California.

Description Thallus calcareous, articulated, light pink, to 10 cm (4 in) tall from a basal crust. Branching pinnate; axial segments flattened, hexagonal in shape, ~1.5 mm (0.06 in) long and 2 mm (0.08 in) wide, slightly wider on branches. This species is found in the low intertidal to upper subtidal rock on exposed shores.

Red bio-band in the low intertidal of Kiska Island, Aleutian Islands.

Species of *Palmaria* on Kodiak Island.

Seagrasses

Phylum Magnoliophyta

Seagrasses are photosynthetic flowering plants occurring worldwide along the coastline from exposed to estuarine habitats (48 species). They form dense beds in suitable Alaska coastal habitats (none are found north of the Seward Peninsula) and may wash up in large amounts following storms or annual diebacks.

Seagrasses are true seed-producing plants, but are not true grasses. They are generally thought to be more closely related to lilies. The basic structural components of seagrasses include rhizomes, which produce roots at intervals known as nodes, and long, ribbonlike leaves, which branch alternately in two rows down the main stem. The flowers are inconspicuous and are often aggregated into spike-like structures at the base of leaf clusters or arranged along elongated shoots.

Specialized traits make seagrasses well adapted to the marine environment. Complex root systems and flexible leaves with air spaces for floatation enable them to handle changing wave energies and water levels. Stomata or holes that allow passage of gases in other vascular plants are lacking. Chloroplasts are present in the epidermis rather than the internal tissues or mesophyll, as in most land plants, allowing photosynthesis to be more efficient when plants are submerged. Reproductive success is assured by pollen being released in gelatinous strands that are carried by water currents to female flowers.

Seagrasses are regarded as highly productive and ecologically valuable organisms. They grow very fast during spring and summer and provide a high caloric, protein-rich diet for animals that eat plants and organic material. Seagrass beds provide habitat for diverse groups of invertebrates, seaweeds, forage fish, waterfowl, and shorebirds, rivaling many other habitat types. There are two main types of seagrasses found in Alaska: surfgrass, commonly associated with exposed rocky beaches, and eelgrass, which inhabits protected, soft sediments.

Serrulated surfgrass
Phyllospadix serrulatus 166

Scouler's surfgrass
Phyllospadix scouleri 168

Eelgrass
Zostera marina 170

Surfgrass

Eelgrass

Serrulated surfgrass
Phyllospadix serrulatus Ruprecht ex Ascherson

Class Liliopsida
Order Alismatales
Family Zosteraceae

North Pacific distribution Chirikof Island and south side of the Alaska Peninsula, Alaska to Cape Arago, Oregon.

Description The long, narrow leaves, to 1 m (39 in) long and 0.8 cm (0.3 in) wide, have serrated margins that can be felt by stroking the leaf margin. The five (or seven) veins running the length of the leaves are the vascular bundles containing xylem and phloem. The leaves are anchored to the substrate by rhizomes; each rhizome node has two roots.

Habitat This species prefers exposed coastlines; it forms a patchwork of beds from mid to low intertidal on rock ramps and boulder fields. Its root system can collect sand, providing a protective habitat for many marine invertebrates.

Similar to See *Phyllospadix scouleri*, which occurs lower in the intertidal and does not extend as far north, and *Zostera marina*, which is found on soft or mixed substrates.

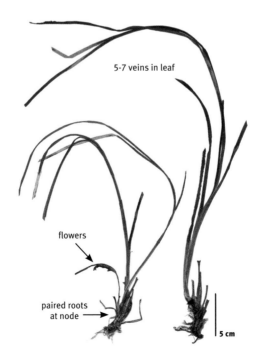

5-7 veins in leaf

flowers

paired roots at node

5 cm

Serrulated surfgrass *Phyllospadix serrulatus*

Serrulated surfgrass beds

Scouler's surfgrass
Phyllospadix scouleri Hooker

Class Liliopsida

Order Alismatales

Family Zosteraceae

North Pacific distribution Sitka Sound, Alaska, to Baja California, Mexico.

Description The long, narrow leaves reach 2 m (6.6 ft) long and 0.5 cm (0.2 in) wide; marginal serrations cannot be felt. Three veins run the length of the leaves. The leaves are anchored to the substrate by rhizomes; each rhizome node has 6-10 roots with fine hairs.

Habitat This species is found in the extreme low intertidal to upper subtidal bedrock on partially to fully exposed shores.

Similar to See *Phyllospadix serrulatus*, which occurs higher in the intertidal and extends farther north, and *Zostera marina*, which is usually found on soft or mixed substrates.

no serrations at margins

3 veins in leaf

6-10 roots at node

5 cm

Scouler's surfgrass *Phyllospadix scouleri*

Flowering Scouler's surfgrass

Eelgrass
Zostera marina Linnaeus

Class Liliopsida

Order Alismatales

Family Zosteraceae

North Pacific distribution Chukchi Sea coast of Alaska to Baja California, Mexico; Korea; Japan; Russia.

Description Leaves are up to 2 m (6.6 ft) long (usually much shorter in Alaska) and 0.15-1.2 cm (0.06-0.5 in) wide. The rhizome is brown and constricted at its nodes, which have many hair-like roots.

Habitat This species usually grows in mud, sand, or gravel, in moderately to fully sheltered areas, from mid intertidal pools into the subtidal. The species provides prime spawning habitat for Pacific herring. Izembek Lagoon, near Bristol Bay, is the largest eelgrass bed in the world.

Similar to *Phyllospadix* spp. are attached to rock, usually bedrock.

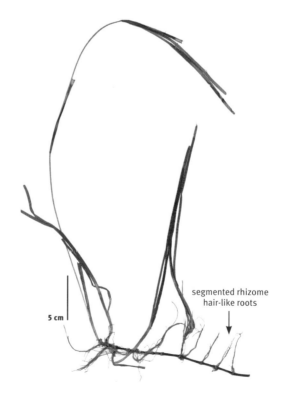

5 cm

segmented rhizome
hair-like roots

Eelgrass *Zostera marina*

Herring roe on eelgrass

Marine Lichens

Kingdom Fungi
Phylum Ascomycota

What is a lichen? Lichens are organisms composed of two, and sometimes three, very different partners. Most of the lichen is the fungal component (the mycobiont), which provides structure and holds water and nutrients. Because fungi can't feed themselves, these "lichenized" fungi have evolved to incorporate photosynthetic green algae; the algae feed the mycobiont by producing carbohydrates (including sugars) from solar energy, water, and carbon dioxide. Some lichens have cyanobacteria (also called blue-green algae) as the photosynthetic component (the photobiont), and some lichens have all three members. Thus, lichens are discrete organisms that have members from at least two (Fungi and Plantae) and/ or a third (Eubacteria) of the currently recognized kingdoms. Lichens are found on all continents, at all elevations, and in the wettest and driest climates. They are perfectly adapted to extreme environments, which often results in slow growth.

There are 15,000 to 20,000 different species of lichens, classified mostly by characteristics of the mycobiont. This is partly due to the complexity of lichen reproduction, where the mycobiont and photobiont(s) must all be present to grow another lichen. Most photobionts can live outside of the lichenized condition, but few of the mycobionts can. This means that the mycobiont must be reunited with a photobiont to survive. The mycobiont is the only partner that reproduces sexually; they do so by producing special sexual spores (ascospores) in sac-like structures (asci) during meiosis. Under favorable conditions an ascospore will germinate, but it must then locate the correct photobiont. Because the mycobiont is the only member that reproduces sexually, lichens are placed in the kingdom Fungi. Lichens are classified by spore and spore production characteristics in addition to morphology.

Asexual reproduction is common and less risky than sexual reproduction because all partners are present in each asexual propagule. Some lichens produce specialized structures that are powdery or grainy (soredia), and others produce shiny outgrowths (isidia and lobules). Some lichens don't produce specialized structures and are simply fragmented by wind, water, animals, or gravity. The various asexual propagules are then transported to new locations by all of these vectors.

Marine lichens are abundant in the high intertidal and supratidal where only the most salt-tolerant species can live. Lichens dominate this extreme zone and are one of the most striking and visible bio-bands in the intertidal. Because all lichens absorb moisture directly from the air, the local distribution of marine lichens is governed primarily by the amount of salt spray exposure they receive. Three common groups of marine lichens, found along Alaska's shoreline, are briefly described here.

White seaside lichen	Black seaside lichen	Orange seaside lichens
Coccotrema maritimum 174	*Verrucaria maura* 176	*Xanthoria* spp. and *Caloplaca* spp. 178

White and black seaside lichens competing for substrate in the supratidal.

Marine Lichens

White seaside lichen
Coccotrema maritimum Brodo

Class Ascomycetes

Order Pertusariales

Family Coccotremataceae

North Pacific distribution Alaska to Washington.

Description Lichen thallus creamy white to pinkish gray. It can be fairly thick and form extensive patches or even bands. Reproductive structures such as soredia are not produced. Visible hemispherical cephalodia (irregular wart-like structures containing cyanobacteria) are scattered across the lichen's surface.

Habitat This lichen will form a white band in the supratidal, frequently on north-facing granitic rock or shaded by overhanging trees, just above the black seaside lichen (*Verrucaria maura* and other *Verrucaria* species).

White seaside lichen, supratidal white band

White seaside lichen *Coccotrema maritimum*

White seaside lichen band

Black seaside lichen

Verrucaria maura Wahlenberg and other *Verrucaria* species

Class Ascomycetes

Order Verrucariales

Family Verrucariaceae

North Pacific distribution Aleutian Islands, Alaska, to Washington.

Description This lichen is by far the most common maritime lichen found on Alaska's coast. The thallus forms extensive black patches that penetrate the surface of siliceous and limestone rocks. They often develop a chinky surface reminiscent of cracked dry mud, or produce low rounded bumps that protrude from the surface. Another species of *Verrucaria* often grows on top of *V. maura*. No reproductive features such as soredia or isidia are produced.

Habitat The species of *Verrucaria* form a striking black band on rock from the high intertidal zone into the supratidal. The lower edge of this band usually marks mean higher high water (MHHW) and the width of the band varies with exposure (less than 1 meter wide in protected areas, and more than 5 meters wide at exposed locations). This lichen is often mistaken for weathered oil.

Black seaside lichen band

Black seaside lichen *Verrucaria maura*

Black seaside lichen band

Orange seaside lichens
Caloplaca spp. and *Xanthoria* spp.

Class Ascomycetes

Order Teloschistales

Family Teloschistinaceae

North Pacific distribution Aleutian Islands, Alaska, to Washington.

Description These two genera produce highly visible light yellow to yolk-yellow, or bright orange to reddish orange blotches on rocks. They form more or less circular patches, which can be powdery to granular, or slightly to distinctly lobed. Many species often produce orange, rimmed, disc-shaped persistent fruiting bodies called apothecia. Some produce granular or powdery soredia on their surface.

Habitat The brilliant yellow-orange color of these lichens on steep, rocky supratidal cliffs along Alaska's coastline can't be missed. Similar-looking species are specialists that can be abundant at seabird rookeries. The bird guano has a high pH and provides lots of nitrogen, calcium, and phosphorus for these lichens.

Orange seaside lichens at supratidal

Orange seaside lichens *Caloplaca* spp. and *Xanthoria* spp.

Orange seaside lichens at supratidal

Selected references

(The following references provide information on seaweeds that was helpful in preparing this guide and that may be useful if you are interested in learning more.)

Abbott, I.A., and G.J. Hollenberg. 1976. Marine algae of California. Stanford University Press, Stanford. 827 pp.

Druehl, L.D. 2000. Pacific seaweeds: A guide to common seaweeds of the west coast. Harbour Publishing, Madeira. 190 pp.

Gabrielson, P.W., T.B. Widdowson, and S.C. Lindstrom. 2006. Keys to the seaweeds and seagrasses of Southeast Alaska, British Columbia, Washington, and Oregon. Phycological Contribution no. 7. PhycoID, Hillsborough. 209 pp.

Garza, D.A. 2005. Common edible seaweeds in the Gulf of Alaska. Alaska Sea Grant College Program, University of Alaska Fairbanks. 57 pp.

Graham, L.E., J.E. Graham, and L.W. Wilcox. 2009. Algae. 2nd edn. Benjamin Cummings (Pearson), San Francisco.

Keeling, P.J., G. Burger, D.G. Durnford, B.F. Lang, R.W. Lee, R.E. Pearlman, A.J. Roger, and M.W. Gray. 2005. The tree of eukaryotes. Trends in Ecology and Evolution 20:670-676. doi:10.1016/j.tree.2005.09.005

Mondragon, J., and J. Mondragon. 2003. Seaweeds of the Pacific Coast: Common marine algae from Alaska to Baja California. Sea Challengers, Monterey. 96 pp.

Murray, S.N., R.E. Ambrose, and M.N. Dethier. 2006. Monitoring rocky shores. University of California Press, Berkeley. 220 pp.

O'Clair, R.M., and S.C. Lindstrom. 2000. North Pacific seaweeds. Plant Press, Auke Bay. 159 pp.

Seaweed resources on the Internet

www.seaweedsofalaska.com
A photo-rich site where much of the material for this book was developed.

www.algaebase.org
AlgaeBase is a database of information on algae that includes terrestrial, marine, and freshwater organisms.

www.beatymuseum.ubc.ca/herbarium/
Home page of the herbarium of the University of British Columbia, which contains a large collection of seaweeds from Alaska.

www.botany.ubc.ca/herbarium/algae/index.html#Projects
This site has data on over 22,000 specimens of seaweeds collected in Alaska and housed in herbaria around the world.

www.alaskafisheries.noaa.gov/habitat/shorezone/szintro.htm
Portal to Alaska ShoreZone coastal habitat mapping and imagery.

Glossary

(Modified from Gabrielson et al. 2006)

alternate branching: with a branch on one side and then on the other side (not opposite) of an axis repeatedly along the axis

annual: living for one year

apical: at the tip of a branch or axis

articulated: jointed

axis: the central, longitudinal element of organization in a plant's architecture

basal: at or toward the base

biennial: living for two years

blade: a flattened leaflike thallus or thallus part

branchlet: a small branch, frequently the ultimate branch in a system of branching

bullate: having a puckered appearance

calcareous: having calcium carbonate; frequently stony

canopy: layers of foliage held above the ocean bottom

carposporangia: sporangia containing the spores formed after fertilization in most higher red algae (Florideophyceae)

chlorophyll: the green photosynthetic pigment found in most photosynthetic organisms

chloroplast: pigmented, photosynthetic organelle (plastid) of eukaryotes

cleft: partly divided or split

coalesced: fused or joined together

conceptacle: a fertile cavity immersed or emergent; may have a pore

confluent: growing together to form a merged mass

conical: cone-shaped

cordate: heart-shaped with the point upward or outward away from the point of attachment

cortex: superficial tissue external to medulla, usually of smaller, pigmented cells

crustose: flattened against the substrate and usually not easily detached

cystocarp: structure on the female gametophyte of red algae composed of diploid tissue (including carposporangia) from fertilization of the female reproductive cell and surrounded by haploid gametophytic tissue; frequently a deeply pigmented macroscopic protrusion (bump) with or without an ostiole (pore)

denticulate: toothed

determinate: having limited growth

diatom: a simple photosynthetic organism, usually a solitary cell, which is encased in a silicon housing

dichotomous branching: branching, often repeatedly, into two more or less equal axes

discoidal: disc-shaped

distal: toward the apex

distichous branching: arranged in two rows on opposite sides of an axis

distromatic: composed of two layers of cells

endemic: restricted to a particular region

ephemeral: short-lived, usually only a few months

epiphytic: growing on a plant, including algae

epizoic: growing on an animal

filamentous: threadlike; sometimes describing thalli only one cell wide

fimbriate: having a fringe

flagella: whiplike cellular appendages used to propel a cell

forcipate: forked like crab pincers

Glossary

fucoxanthin: a photosynthetic pigment that gives brown seaweeds their brown color

gametophyte: haploid, gamete-producing plant in an alternation of generations life history

gamete: a cell that fuses with another cell in sexual reproduction

gland cell: colorless, usually refractive (shiny) cell with apparently homogeneous contents, in contrast to neighboring pigmented cells that have structured contents (Rhodophyta)

haptera: the branched root-like parts of a holdfast

herbivore: plant eater

heteromorphic: having two different morphologies

holdfast: structure by which an alga attaches to the substrate

indeterminate: having unlimited growth

intertidal: shore area between high and low tide marks

irregular branching: branches not inserted along an axis in any particular pattern

isomorphic: having similar morphologies

kelp: large plants (sporophyte generation) belonging to the brown algal order Laminariales

lacerated: irregularly cleft or cut; torn along the margin

laminarin: a storage product (polysaccharide) found within the cells of brown algae

lanceolate: lance-shaped; narrow and tapering

lateral: to the side

ligulate: strap-shaped

mastigoneme: a fine, microscopic hair-like structure on a flagellum (Phaeophyceae)

medulla: central core of tissue in a multicellular alga, frequently differentiated from the cortex and usually colorless (lacking photosynthetic pigments)

meiospore: a haploid cell produced by meiosis that gives rise to a gametophyte by mitotic cell division

meristem: group or region of rapidly dividing cells that initiate growth

midrib: thickened central axis of a flattened thallus

monostromatic: composed of a single layer of cells

mucilage duct: intercellular space in cortex of stipe and/or blade of some Laminariales (Phaeophyceae) lined by secretory cells that produce and secrete fucoidin

mucilaginous: slimy

multinucleate: having more than one nucleus in a cell

mycobiont: fungal component of a lichen

opposite branching: arrangement where each branch of a pair is directly across (180 degrees) from the other branch

palmate: resembling a hand with the fingers spread

papillae: short, nipple-like outgrowths on the surface

pectinate branching: having branches all on one side of an axis, resembling a comb

perennial: living for more than two years

perforated: having holes

pericentral cells: cut off from central, axial cells

phase: the gametophyte or sporophyte generation in an organism that undergoes alternation of generations

photobiont: photosynthetic component of a lichen

phycology: the study of algae, including seaweeds

pinnate branching: feather-like; branching opposite, profuse, equal, and distichous

pit plugs (connections): appearing as a dumbbell-shaped structure or as a cytoplasmic connection linking adjacent cells (Rhodophyta), seen with a light microscope

pluriseriate: arranged in two or more rows

pneumatocyst: an air bladder or float (Phaeophyceae)

polysiphonous: consisting of a central file of cells surrounded by additional files of cells of the same height

polysporangia: sporangia containing more than four (usually many) spores (Rhodophyta), typically the products of meiosis followed by mitosis

proliferous: bearing numerous additional parts

propagule: a multicellular structure that propagates a plant vegetatively

protuberance: knob

pyrenoid: refractive (shiny) body frequently seen in plastids

radial: arrangement of parts in many directions relative to a central axis, like the spokes of a wheel

receptacle: inflated branch tip or branchlet that contains conceptacles (Phaeophyceae, Fucales)

reticulate: with a network of veins

rhizoidal branch: a colorless, multicellular filament that attaches a plant to the substrate or one part of a plant to another

saccate: sac-like, hollow

serrate: toothed on the margins like a saw

sinusoidal: S-shaped

sori: cluster of reproductive structures, sometimes appearing distinct on the plant surface

spatulate: obovate apically with a long attenuate base; spoon-shaped

spermatangia: reproductive cells in which nonflagellated male gametes (spermatia) are formed (Rhodophyta)

sporangia: structures in which spores (non-gamete reproductive cells) are borne

sporophyte: the diploid plant in an alternation of generations life history; the phase in which meiosis occurs in a sporangium to produce haploid spores

sporophyll: specialized blade that bears sporangia (Phaeophyceae)

stipe: elongate, terete, or compressed part of thallus between holdfast and blade

substrate: the base on which an organism lives, such as rock, wood, animals, or other plants

subtidal: shore area below extreme lower low water

supratidal: shore area above the high-tide mark

taxon (sing.), taxa (pl.): a unit in the classification of organisms; (in descending order of hierarchy) phylum, class, order, family, genus, species

terete: cylindrical but somewhat tapered distally

terminal: at the end of a structure

tetrasporangia: sporangia containing four spores, usually the products of meiosis

tetrasporophyte: the diploid, tetrasporangia-producing phase in higher red algae (Florideophyceae)

thallus (sing.), thalli (pl.): plant body typically lacking differentiated tissue such as roots, stems, or leaves

Glossary

trichoblast: unbranched or branched, unpigmented, filamentous branchlet typically evident at branch apices (Rhodomelaceae, Rhodophyta)

tubular: shaped like a hollow cylinder

undulate: wavy

unilateral: occurring only on one side of an axis

uniseriate: having a single file of cells

vein: macroscopically a noticeable line of thickening in a blade; microscopically a file (or files) of cells that are longer, thicker, or both compared to adjacent cells

verrucose: covered with tubercles or warts

verticillate: whorled

whorled: having three or more branches at a node

zygotosporangia: sporangia containing the spores formed after fertilization in the Bangiales (Rhodophyta)

Index to common and scientific names

Index to common and scientific names

186

Index to common and scientific names

Index to common and scientific names